# THE WAY HOME

## A PLEIADIAN LIFE-LINE FOR HUMANITY IN CRISIS

PAULA HART

Arcadia Press

**The Way Home**

A Pleiadian Life-line for Humanity in Crisis

© Copyright Paula Hart 2019

All rights reserved.

Published 2019

ISBN 978-0-6483772-2-1

Published by Arcadia Press

www.arcadiapress.com.au

Country of publication: Australia

*Disclaimer:* This book is made available with the
understanding that its contents contain the ideas and
opinions of its author and contributor and that these ideas
and opinions should not be construed as medical advice
for any individual, their condition or life situation. The
reader is also encouraged to seek the advice and support
of their trusted health care professionals where required.

Arcadia Press

**The Way Home**

A Pleiadian Life-line for Humanity in Crisis

© Copyright Paula Hart 2019

Published 2019

ISBN 978-0-6483772-2-1

Published by Arcadia Press

www.arcadiapress.com.au

Country of publication: Australia

*Disclaimer:* This book is made available with the
understanding that its contents contain the ideas and
opinions of its author and contributor and that these ideas
and opinions should not be construed as medical advice
for any individual, their condition or life situation. The
reader is also encouraged to seek the advice and support
of their trusted health care professionals where required.

# Contents

## CHAPTER 8

## CHAPTER 9

## CHAPTER 10

## CHAPTER 11

# Introduction

During the 1990's, my life changed with accelerating speed. In 1995 I changed my working identity from occupational therapist to Feng Shui consultant. Shortly after, I found I could obtain useful answers to my questions both from a dowsing rod and from intuitive or channelled writing. When I encountered difficulties relating to my teenaged children, my work or life direction, I learnt to type my questions into the computer and wait. Amazingly, very wise answers would usually be provided, and I would end up gazing at the computer screen in awe. The answers often seemed to point to a much broader picture than the focus of my immediate concerns.

On 1st July, 1997, I watched a documentary on television that examined the possibilities and potential for biological warfare, and the Western world's lack of preparation for such an eventuality. The images shown of the effects of anthrax and other such horrific germs sickened me, and sent me racing to the computer for some answers. This book seems to be the result.

Before I started the book I was told:

"The forces of light will always ultimately overcome. It is all a matter of time, since you have created this concept in which to live. It is a matter of how much the light forces can prevent the dark forces from doing damage in the time before they are overcome. Whatever happens on Earth is reflected elsewhere in the universe, and echoes follow us all. We do not wish to be a part of the destructive experiment of competition, which your people are playing out, but, as members of the same universe, we have no choice. Therefore, please let others know that we are here, and that their actions affect more than those whom they can conquer. We have the capacity to stop the unwise actions on Earth in a forthright manner, but this is not how we operate. We choose to co-operate rather than conquer – even at grave risk to our wellbeing. We learnt long ago that to conquer is to lose. Our message to you is one of peace, love and concern.

We come from a small group of stars called the Pleiades. And from Orion. You may call us The Others. However, you have amongst you others from other places – some not as well meaning as ourselves. We would ask you to regard them all with love. This will counteract any undesirable influence they could have upon you. Remember, love is the ultimate protection, through which no evil can penetrate. We ask you not to bow down to any influence, but to judge for yourself what is right, for you will always know.

We believe your people can best understand information in story form. Your stories usually begin with 'once upon a time.' So that is how we will begin.

This will be your introduction:

Once upon a time, there was a giant who had nowhere to go. He had much potential, but had no way to use it; was full of vision, but with nothing to see; full of love, with nothing to shower it on. His longing created a seed, and this seed exploded into a thousand billion whirling fragments, which gradually formed clusters and sparks. The sparks became human souls, and the clusters became the stars and planets of the galaxies.

The giant had created his world. He looked into it in wonder and beheld such beauty that he decided he would never change it. He would merely love it and track its path with the greatest interest.

As he watched, the sparks and clusters began to interact. Some sparks grew brighter and others dimmer; the clusters developed different characteristics and attracted different sparks. The sparks lived off the clusters like parasites and, as he watched, the giant was dismayed to find some clusters being slowly destroyed by the very sparks they were nurturing. He longed to intervene, but was bound by his promise of non-interference. It seemed to him that the dimmer the sparks became, the more damage they did to their host cluster and, even more strangely, to each other.

The giant's distress was felt by the brighter sparks, who were still connected to him. They sensed his need for intervention, and came from all sides to help. There was a feeling that time may run out for some clusters, and Earth was one of them."

A couple of nights later this message came through. I was told it was from the Brotherhood of Light:

"Our purpose is ultimately to have some influence

over what happens here on Earth, through blending our consciousness with yours. We believe this to be in both our interests. We will gain confidence about the security of the Earth's future and its effects on us, and you will gain depth of spirit, power, health and connection.

That music you are playing, you are using it to manipulate your consciousness – to affect it and influence its state. What we are doing is no more sinister than that. We are, in a sense, implanting the music of the universe into you, because your species lost it long ago and has never refined the use of it as we have. We would like the Earth to be able to create the tune of her longing, instead of crying out in pain as she does now. In order for this to happen, we must influence Earth's caretakers – human beings.

Human beings have created systems which have born you away from yourselves and from the deeper reality. Economic systems, social systems, religious systems, technological systems, each useful to you in its own way, but also equally seductive. Humankind's consciousness has not developed finely enough overall to be able to deal with the pressures of these systems, and the valve on the pressure cooker, so to speak, is your mother, the Earth. She pays the price for the developments which seem to make your lives easier. But, so do you. For as long as some are rich, many thousands will be poor; as long as there are religions, there will be divisions; as long as there is an economic system, there is no spontaneous sharing; as long as there is technology, humans cannot rest, content in what they already have. Inequality breeds hatred,

hatred breeds fear, and fear distorts love – the matter of the universe. Greed is born of a sense of lack, and is by nature never satisfied.

We ask you not to dismantle the fabric of your societies, but to weave some new strands into them – strands of humility, compassion, generosity, awareness and vision. And most of all love, a commodity that is reserved by most humans for favoured family members and friends. You do not know how you deprive yourselves in doing this. This selective notion of love is the creator of loneliness, of stilted affections, of jealousy and revenge. It is the father of genocide and racism, the mother of depression.

The truth that seems to elude most of mankind is that there is love everywhere, enough for everyone. Love is not exclusive, does not depend on identity, deeds or appearance. Love is not limited in quantity – it does not run dry. All you have to do is tap into it, and it will refresh you, whoever you are. That is the promise of love, and that is the truth. This love is what you know of as qi, or life force.

Most of your people believe this life force can only be gained from other people, and this belief is the foundation of many of your problems. Love is in you and around you, all the time, accessible unless you refuse it. All you have to do is stop and feel it, to know.

We are telling you all this so that you will understand where we are coming from, and what our aims are. So you will understand that we come from the same sparks as you. We just flew a little further.

At the same time as we work with you and other

individuals, many others are working with the mass consciousness of humankind. Our goal is the development of a human race that can see itself and the consequences of its deeds, and not be too proud or afraid to rectify its mistakes.

We were never meant to be your allies, but your friends. The difference is that while allies support each other in time of need or crisis, friends are always there for each other, helping and sharing in daily experiences – happy as well as sad. We are always there for you in this way. Please do not wait for crises to communicate with us, for we would be of service and friendship long before that.

Secondly, we would never wish to declare ourselves to be in line with your defence personnel, for where one defends, another must be attacking, or thought to be doing so. We wish to distance ourselves from such a scenario, for it is not our interest to be divisive, or to interpret events in divisive ways.

Rather, we would advise, if requested to do so, on strategies of response to such situations. The strategies we would advise are ones that would take into account the needs of humankind – rather than of one specific race or group. This is because ultimately the group and the whole are synonymous.

So, in this present case, where there is much grief, loss and suffering on the part of some, and much fear and loathing on the part of others, we would advise caution. This caution would be best held until a reasonable amount of understanding is in place, between the conflicted parties. The understanding would need to cover such elements as a depth of feeling for the other's misfortune, a sorrow for one's own part in this, and a resolve to make things better for all concerned. If caution is not held until this point, war will be inevitable. War is such a sorry concept. The battle itself is the only winner ultimately. All other parties are diminished as they struggle to come to terms with the roles they have played, and the losses they have incurred and have foist upon others. We beg you to consider your options carefully and lengthily before making forceful decisions. You have seen the effects of war. "

The Pleiades is a group of stars I knew little about. The Pleiades has always intrigued humanity, and it seems, the Pleiadians have always had an interest in Earth. Mayan legend has it that the constellation of the Pleiades was formed as a result of a massacre. Long ago, before there was a sun, Gukup Cakix, a giant, pretended to be the sun and the moon. However this was known to be untrue, as Gukup was a vain and cruel creature. Two brothers, with their grandparents help, eventually managed to punish and kill Gukup and his wife. However the two sons of the giant remained. Zipacna, the elder son, was asked by a group of youths to dig a hole supposedly for a tree. Their plan was to make Zipacna climb into the hole, then bury him. However, the giant tricked them, and escaped through a tunnel. When the youths were drunk from celebrating their victory over him, Zipacna massacred them. The young ones were changed into the constellation of stars known as the Pleiades.

Another reference to the Pleiades is made in Hottentot mythology. The supreme god of the Hottentots is Tsui-Goab, a great priest and sorcerer, who lives in the Red Sky. He commands storms, sends rain for crops and speaks with the voice of thunder. The adversary of Tsui-Goab is Gaunab, chief of the dead, who lives in the Black Sky. Tsui-Goab kills Gaunab, but is first wounded in the knee during a fight. His name means "Wounded Knee". The cult of Tsui-Goab is celebrated when the Pleiades appear.[1]

Greek mythology has it that the Pleiades are the seven daughters of Atlas and the nymph Pleione. They committed suicide due to their distress at the death of one of their number. Zeus then placed them in the sky as a cluster of seven stars. One of the stars, Merope, is fainter than the others, because of her shame at having once loved a mortal.

During the Aboriginal Dreamtime, Wati-kutjara, the two lizard men saved a group of women from Kulu, the moon man. The lizard men wounded Kulu with their magical boomerang, and he died thereafter, possibly causing the moon to be pale ever since. The saved women chose to leave the earth and become the Pleiades. The lizard men became the Gemini constellation.[2]

According to Greek mythology again, Hermes, who later became the patron of all magicians and scientists, was the son of Zeus and Maia. Maia was a nymph on

1 Larousse – *World Mythology* 1965, Hamlyn Publishing group

2 Arthur Cotterell – *The Illustrated Encyclopaedia of Myths and Legends* 1989, Collins Publishers Australia

earth, and is the middle star of the Pleiades.

Perhaps the most interesting and relevant reference to the Pleiades comes from Peru. In many lands, the Pleiades were associated with the beginning of the new year and the ending of the old one. In Peru an annual ceremony of penitence and sadness was held just before the sun reached its highest point in the sky. At this time the Pleiades passed through the zenith at midnight, when they were opposite the sun. This Ayamarca ceremony was held in November, a month which, in northern countries reminded people of old age and death. They were aware, however that it merely signified change: death would be replaced by new life. Even though in Peru the seasons did not echo those in the northern hemisphere, the Peruvians saw November as a time to cleanse the country from sin, and to appease the powers of nature. Rituals were held to purify the city, as well as the individuals. After much sorrow, it was hoped the gods would accept their offerings and a new and better future would be forthcoming.[3]

I had always had an open mind about extraterrestrials, thanks to my mother, who was constantly ribbed by the family for her interest in outlandish, esoteric things. Although I too have had numerous 'experiences' over the years, perhaps one of the strongest signs of their presence was a strange line that appeared overnight across my back lawn. It was about 6–10 centimetres wide and formed by completely flattened grass. Friends offered different opinions on what could have made this line, which

3 C. A. Burland – *Myths of Life and Death* 1974, Macmillan

even showed up in the moonlight as a silvery ribbon. Could it be from the dog running up and down, or perhaps a burglar had pulled a very heavy bag of stolen booty across the lawn? It was still evident after the lawn was mowed, and disappeared only after three or four weeks.

UFO? I don't know, but I can't think of a more likely explanation. Soon after this I was asked to take my 'computer writing questions' to the next level and write this book. Initially it was hard work, not finishing their sentences for them as I saw fit. Eventually, they politely thanked me for my efforts at interpreting for them, but said there was no need – I should just write down what they told me. I would get most of the words clearly, but at times just a concept, which I would have to put into words. Writing the book was a moving experience. At times I sensed the urgency of their concern, for which I could find no equivalent words. I grappled with my rational mind, my doubts and fears, and a dislike of the word "channelling", for its connotation of New Age charlatanism.

At times the messages seemed so relevant to me that I wondered if they were meant specifically for me, but was reassured that they were universal. Sometimes I feared they were contradicting themselves, then realised that they were offering information in ways they felt we might best understand. They were also clearly not wanting to or able to answer every one of our questions about our creation and existence. Their mission was to help us in our understanding, in order to facilitate our wiser decision-making.

What you have now in your hands is the result of

my communications with the Pleiadians. May it serve you well.

*Paula Hart*

MELBOURNE 2019

CHAPTER 1

# In the beginning...

The story began long ago, and it began with a bang. Becoming wise is a life-long process. And so it is with the Earth. She spins unswervingly until she completes her cycle. Then it is time for a change, for the journey to the next stage of her evolution.

A change is needed to enable the survival of all concerned. And it is not a change anyone relishes. The Earth has now almost completed her cycle, and she is becoming wise.

Humankind, below the stars, and planted on the Earth, wonders what will become of it and its mother, the Earth. There are dreams of catastrophe and dreams of utopia; fears of genocide and hopes for peace. Humankind, within its self-created mist, cannot see beyond.

But there are others who are able to pierce the veil of time. We wish to show you what we see, we would fuel your hopes, feed your dreams and share your joy. We want you to know what lies beyond.

It is not yourselves alone who are affected by your actions, fears and thoughts. We, too, are here, and although you cannot see us, we have communicated many times with you. Our desire is that you overcome your fears about our very existence, and realise that we are gentler beings than you yourselves. We mean no harm, and only wish to open your eyes to the greater whole in which you live, unaware. For should you not understand soon, we may all be headed for a less fruitful existence than the one we now enjoy.

So in this book, we wish to take you on a journey of discovery and learning. A journey which may surprise, enlighten and refresh you, and draw you closer to your soul.

## Separation and the birth of desires

To begin:

There was a time when man did not know himself as separate – when he went along with the crowd, as a cell in an organism. He had no notion of what it was to be independent, and would have greatly feared and abhorred the idea. Over many, many years, this primitive man's consciousness evolved, until he reached a stage in which he could comprehend the basics of separateness. He slowly understood that he had a mind of his own and could form decisions based on his own desires.

As he discovered his power, he began to separate himself from the rhythms of the Earth, which had truly been his nurturer in the past. He began to put his desires ahead of his understanding of the seasons, of the directions and tides. And that is when he began to forget. In separating himself from his Mother, he started to forget who gave him life.

As he continued on his journey, he developed more faith in his own ideas and feelings as an individual. His deep roots into the earth and his respect for nature gradually withered, and were scoffed at and scorned. Much of man's knowledge and connection with nature was transferred into the realms of mythology. Those who insisted on the validity of the old ways were rejected in favour of adherence to man's developing perception of his dominion over all of creation.

Man's ego replaced his connection with nature. Instead of accepting Earth's nurturing, he sought satisfaction through gratifying his desires. This kind of satisfaction is but a short-lived, illusory, hollow one, causing man to strive ever harder to achieve his aims.

In becoming separate from nature, man began to weaken his ties to all life, and soon conflict began – between families, tribes and nations. In order to fulfil ever-increasing desires, men conquered each other, trying to capture satisfaction in the form of land, goods and pleasure. Hollow victories indeed.

(What we are showing you at this stage is how humankind reached current times. Then we will show you how current problems can be corrected, as we see it.)

## Forgetting and the birth of technology

Parallel to this development was the beginning of technology and other systems. Without direct access to love energy (life force) from the universe via Earth, man tried vainly to find ways to achieve contentment and health. Regulation of his behaviour and thoughts seemed important, so he created religion, as a framework. Mastery over time and space seemed necessary, so he invented technologies which would enable him to achieve more in less time. Suffering and death were looked upon unfavourably, as almost unnatural, and medical systems were forged to cheat disease and to prolong life. The notions of trust and honest sharing of assets and resources died, and were replaced with a fierce economic system, in which only the fittest survived.

Somewhere in all this, man lost much of the connection with his soul.

Even as man talked about the world becoming smaller with the advent of ever more effective means of travel, so it also became more divided and less tolerant. What we found hard to comprehend was that an increase in travel did not correlate more with an increase in the growth of understanding and appreciation of differences.

Of course, the global only reflects the individual, and vice versa. So, within each individual grew greed, conflict and the great forgetfulness of where he had come from. And what would you do if you found yourself lost in a foreign land? You would probably do just what humankind did: try to make the most of it. Since you had no one really on your side (or so you thought), you would make sure you got your share.

This is what nations and individuals have been doing for millennia now, to the detriment of themselves and their planet.

## The cycle of return

Now is the end of that cycle. The cycle of separateness is turning. Soon man will once again find himself and his true origins. If that is hard to understand, imagine this: A toddler walks away from her mother in a park. As she walks away, she gets further and further out of her mother's sight and reach. She walks on and on. As she walks, she grows taller, becoming a child, then an adolescent. She walks on, becoming an adult, and as she has walked around the Earth, she eventually arrives back at her mother, whence she started.

All life moves in cycles, and man's consciousness is no exception.

So it is time for man to come home again.

We know this has been told to you – the same people who listen to such messages again and again. So we do not claim to be messengers of a fresh truth, but a truth it is nonetheless, and we would have you hear and understand it for the happy news it is.

Many of you believe the tales of woe and disaster which have been spelled out for you by various prophets of doom. We ask you not to give these tales credence, lest you unwittingly create them. It is true that you all, no matter how hypocritical, live by your beliefs. For you create in your lives what you believe will happen. There are many levels of belief, and it is your deepest beliefs that hold the most power.

We beg you to believe in a peaceful transition, a harmonious return of the prodigal sons and daughters. Do not imagine that you are the only beings who have endured this cycle. There are many, many before you who have been through similar changes. Some were successful, and some not so. Our endeavours are to help you join the former group.

If you resist nature, and deny the moves necessary for the change, you will be pushing nature past the barriers of her capability. This would be a tragedy for us all. By this we mean for more than just you and ourselves. There are indeed many others watching your progress with some anxiety and concern.

Having divorced yourselves from nature, most of you are unable to grasp the interconnectedness of all life. It is but an abstract concept for many of you. However, there are many of us to whom it is a crucial reality, and we are somewhat dependent upon your well-being and that of the Earth.

You ask who we are? We are a group of representatives from the stars you know as the Pleiades. We are asking you to uncover your eyes, and to peek even just for an instant, at the reality of your state. After that, you may decide what you will do.

We put to you two scenarios:

One is of a woman gathering water at a well. She bends down, lowers her water urn, and is suddenly surprised by a snake. She puts down her urn calmly, and gently croons to the snake, who is charmed. She strokes the snake then it slithers away. She resumes her water-collecting, reflecting upon her experience.

The other scene is of another woman at the well. When she sees the snake she shrieks, panics, drops the urn and it breaks. The snake gets a fright, rears and bites her on the wrist. Now she cannot collect water, with a poisoned arm and a broken urn. She cries out in agony.

What is the difference between these two women, you ask? One woman accepts what is nature, the other resists. Acceptance breeds acceptance, while resistance causes pain. If humankind understood this simple principle, we would probably not have needed to be here today.

If mankind can understand that a change is now needed in order to complete the cycle gracefully, all will be well. What is needed is a realistic look at what man has achieved and what he has not achieved.

It is of deep concern for us that man is forgetting who he really came here to be.

## The experiment of time and space

Man was put on Earth for a grand experiment – the experiment of time and space, of experience and finiteness. The plan was that man would be able to be God in form, to create the fabric of God's imaginings, if you will allow some poetic licence. This, of course, is what has been happening, but somewhere along the space-time bar, man began to do things which endanger the whole. God will not and may not intervene, but we, as a part of the greater whole, may and are coming in to help. Our task is not to change you against your will, but to enhance your consciousness in the gentlest possible way, so that you are more able to make decisions that will serve you well. In so doing, we are trying to ensure that this magnificent experiment does not become too irrevocably altered.

But, you say, there are massive changes happening in the universe all the time – what does one more change matter overall? The answer to that is that this one matters, because this little part of the universe is very special. You do not realise how extraordinarily beautiful it is in comparison with most others. You do not realise how special you are as beings, compared with others. Earth beings are gifted in a wonderful way. They have the power of emotions. We do not have this gift. We are only capable of love and cannot feel the range of feelings you do. Other beings do not have your soul. They may have technology far superior to yours, but they cannot discriminate in matters of conscience, and do not have depth in relationships.

## Earth – The exceptional mother

How is it that man got to be so lucky? Because his were the original sparks that came to Earth, and Earth was an exceptional mother. Some environments provided their sparks with the materials for shelter, and the barest of essentials only. This is why many of those beings have since developed amazingly advanced space technology – they wanted to get out and find somewhere better. (They did. They found Earth. But more of that later.) Some environments provided a different sort of energy, which fostered beings in different dimensions, invisible to most human beings.

And then there was Earth, which surrounded its sparks in such a rainbow of beauty and abundance that they could not fail to thrive. Through constant exposure to the endless natural richness of sensory stimulation: the music of the wind, waves and birds, awe-inspiring scenery to microscopic wonders, the delicious variety of tastes and textures, man was moved to develop an equally wide array of emotions, depths, and capacities.

Man's cultural achievements illustrate this capacity. These achievements are unparalleled anywhere in the universe. You were driven to recreate the magnificence of the sunsets, through painting and music; you tried to copy wildlife in sculptures; and you created stories to explain what you could not really understand. The extremes of beauty and expression of your mother meant that you too were driven to extremes of agonising joy and pathos.

This is where we return to the beginning of the story. While you acknowledged that your primary relationship was with the Earth, all was well. Perhaps you didn't have brick houses, aeroplanes or antigens, but you had a sense of security and connection; of being nurtured as part of something greater. By your standards now, it was a simple time, of glorying at the night sky, of breathing to Earth's rhythms, of wandering and wonder.

It was sufficient – well almost. There was a crack in the system, and that was man's own ingenuity. Earth mothered him well, and gave him many opportunities to create, to invent and to solve problems. As man grew in these capacities, so did his imagination. He learnt other ways from the creatures he saw, and took lessons from nature. Not only did he solve his survival problems of food and shelter, but his imagination extended his ideas of what quality of life meant. One could say he became unsatisfied with having everything, and wanted more, not realising he had it all already. So, instead of eating to fill his belly, he chose certain flavours; instead of sleeping where he happened to be, he built special places which he could embellish more and more, and called them home; instead of loving everyone equally, he chose a few whom he liked best.

Increasingly, man was motivated by desires, rather than by life itself. In fulfilling his desires, man often had to step out of rhythm with the Earth. Yes, this was indeed man's toddler era – the beginning of his independence. And the beginning of his forgetting. As he went about his business, doing what he wanted to do, he started to forget how he had relied upon Earth for all his gifts. He began to manufacture what he wanted for himself, using materials from Earth, without asking permission. He gradually began subjugating his mother to his own desires. Her minerals were dragged out of her, her tree coating was burnt or torn off to make more space for man, her rivers were polluted, her creatures tortured or killed. Her breath was choked, and in some areas even her cells were altered by weapons of war. She was cut, scarred and drilled for the sake of transport and buildings. The delicate but robust balance she had maintained for so long, was threatened. That balance is now teetering.

Many of you suspect that Earth, like man, has feelings and is planning some sort of nasty revenge for all that man has done to her. This is not so. The Earth, although she is your mother, is a giant organism, subject to cycles and order. Originally, this order was exquisite and self-sustaining. Earth could even put up with abuse and self-correct the results. But a state has been reached wherein so much of the order has been destroyed that Earth cannot self-correct. The cycles and rhythms are on the brink of losing their regularity. The basic substance on which the Earth depends has become mutilated, to the extent that this organism is almost running out of life, as any organism would under such circumstances.

One could say that the main elements of Earth's life were air, light, minerals and water, but one would be missing the point. The main element of life, as some physicists are now discovering, is love. Love is energy and energy is love. Any other emotions are fostered by desire. Love is not in fact an emotion. It is life.

## The beginning of greed

The former close relationship between man and Earth was nurturing and energising for them both. Man respected and appreciated Earth, which assisted her energy and her ability to maintain her equilibrium. In turn she looked after man's every need. With the dissolution of the respect has come struggle, for both parties. Man's balance has become skewed towards a philosophy of greed, at the expense of its majority; and Earth has been thrown towards natural disasters of unprecedented magnitude in attempting to regain her balance.

It is a sad scenario. But with understanding and

change on man's part, the landscape can be changed into one of beauty and peace.

At the beginning of this chapter, we mentioned the long cycle which is now coming to an end. You may find this confusing in the light of this most recent discussion. This is the natural cycle, which would have been journeyed by Earth whatever man did or did not do. It is one of the longer of Earth's many cycles. Students of astrology understand these cycles well. As bodies have reproductive, digestive and birth/ death cycles, so the Earth has day/ night; seasonal cycles, and many others. The current long cycle leads to a significant cleansing ritual, in which Earth rids herself of major toxins accumulated during that time, in an effort to heal herself before the start of a new cycle. Obviously, the greater the toxic load Earth carries, the greater the cleansing process has to be. Perhaps you are now beginning to understand?

The small differences between you as people – the colours, beliefs, nationalities, the injustices and inequalities – are all largely insignificant in the face of what lies before you as a species.

## A stressed planet

A decision needs to be made, and it needs to be made by as many of you as possible as quickly as possible. Will humans behave as Earth's vermin, feeding off her while infecting her? Or will you choose to be Earth's sons and daughters – here in an interdependent, caring and respectful relationship?

At this crucial point in humankind's the Earth's

evolution, Earth desperately needs your love to energise her and help her self-correct, before that cleansing time escalates.

Your planet is now so stressed that if the pressures on her are to continue as they are now for a few more years, we do not know whether her cleansing cycle will be successful, or lead to disintegration.

This may be alarming news, but we do not wish to distress or frighten you. Our aim is to lift the blinkers from your eyes in time for you to act. For there is much you can do to salvage this situation.

CHAPTER 2

# So little time, so much to do.

## The balance of space and matter

"Let there be spaces in your togetherness", wrote Kahlil Gibran. One could say that this is the key to life on Earth. If togetherness is matter with matter, people with people, and atoms with atoms, the space between carries the love that conditions those atoms, people and materials. The space between is certainly as important as matter itself; in fact, matter depends on it. One can interpret this truism on any scale, from universal space to the space around a nucleus, to the space in the mind of a person. Without the correct relationship between matter and space, balance is lost.

This fact is man's saving grace, as it is an imbalance he can rectify easily.

Over the past 2000 years humans have gradually become obsessed with matter and have denied the space of existence. Man has spent billions of dollars exploring outer space, but has not recognised that he has largely closed off his inner space exploration. He has taught his young to interact with matter, to think rationally and to banish dreams. He prizes doing and deplores being, because this is what suits the systems he has created.

## Doing versus being

Today, those who want to explore the state of just "being" tend to be judged, shunned, pressured into action and guilt-ridden. Unless they wear monks' robes, they are treated as ill or unwilling. However, they are the balance man needs. They are your natural, organic, community self-correction mechanism. They should be supported in their "being", as this is their purpose. If they, too, are forced into action, it will be to man's detriment.

Point number one: allow those people to "be", and in being, they will help rebalance your community, which, in turn will help the Earth.

The reason these special people have come to do your being for you, is that not enough of you are setting aside time to do so yourselves. The faster life seems to become for you, the more you do; but the more you do, the more you need to be, to balance yourself. This seems to be contrary to what you have taught each other.

How to just be? It is so simple. Just stop doing. That means stop acting, moving, talking, thinking. That is all there is to it! The Eastern lands have held understanding of this need for a long time, and we have tried to assist the filtration of their knowledge to the West over many decades. Many meditation techniques have been sampled, and later dropped due to lack of time. It is not lack of time that is the culprit, but lack of understanding. Lack of time is the result of lack of space – made in your days and in your minds – and will be the result for all on Earth if changes are not made more quickly. We urge you to take this seriously and to act, or rather, not act on it!

For those of you who do not know how to stop, here is a simple technique. When you practise it remember that you are performing a service not only for yourself, but for all of humankind, and even Earth herself. Often the simplest acts are the most powerful in creating change, and there is immense power in space, which is harnessed when you open yourself to it.

# THE SPACE TECHNIQUE (exercise)

## Version 1 (exercise)

Familiarise yourself with the technique before you attempt to try it.

You need only set aside 5 minutes, but may prefer to spend up to half an hour.

---

*Lie on your back, under the stars, or imagine the stars above you as you lie on your bed. Squint your eyes a little and focus on a particular star until it goes blurry. Then close your eyes and imagine yourself on that star......*
*all around is light, as you saw from below......*
*Now imagine yourself blending with that light......*
*and actually becoming that star......*
*You are the star......*
*and you can feel that light throughout your*

*being......*
*light inside and around you......*
*float in the experience of that light......*
*Now travel from the centre of that light to the edge,*
*and become aware of the darkness all around......*
*a huge dark void, warm and velvety......*
*gently float out of the light and into that welcoming*
*darkness......*
*you feel yourself expanding......*
*there are no boundaries here......*
*and you can expand infinitely......*
*all barriers dropping away as you expand into*
*endless space and perfect peace......*
*Return to conscious awareness of the depth of calm*
*and the expansion you feel......*
*Become aware of how your body feels......*
*Now slowly open your eyes.*

---

Different people have different associations and preferences, so we offer a variation.

## Version 2 (exercise)

---

*Lie on your back in bed. Get warm and comfortable.*
*You may sit if you prefer. Close your eyes and notice*
*how things look inside your closed eyes......dark and*
*velvety......*
*Notice that there is nothing there to see......*
*all the usual exterior things are shut out......*
*and you are here in a quiet peaceful place......*
*with nothing to respond to......*
*just being aware of this calm, dark space......*

*and now blending with the darkness......*
*becoming the darkness......*
*and the peace......*
*and becoming aware that the darkness is turning into*
*light......*
*first distant and dim......*
*then gradually becoming brighter......*
*and brighter......*
*You are that light......*
*and you can feel it through your being......*
*and the energy of it surging through you......*
*until it becomes dazzling......*
*exploding through your whole being in a joyous*
*burst......*
*You feel yourself expanded......*
*and energised......*
*and light......*
*Return to conscious awareness of the lightness you*
*feel, the calmness and expansion......*
*notice how your body feels......*
*slowly open your eyes.*

———————————

If 10 million of the Earth's population were to follow one of these exercises for just 5 minutes each, twice a day, the world would change radically for the better, and quickly, and many of the disasters man has forecast would be eradicated from your future.

That is all it would take.

CHAPTER 3

# We come not to crown Caesar, but to bury him.

## Greatness

Humankind has never honoured its great leaders. Throughout your history, most of your great leaders have not been acknowledged. Instead, they have been tormented, belittled and put to death. Why, you ask? Because man cannot recognise his own greatness, his capacity for expansion. And when someone comes along who can expand into the greater being that you were all designed to be, others are frightened by this possibility. The great person is quickly cut down to size so that no comparisons can be made and ultimately, no hypotheses formulated about what man really is capable of.

Nelson Mandela's greatness shone through adversity and politics, and his integrity and courage afforded him public credibility. When, after 27 years of imprisonment, he became president of his nation, he spoke some very pertinent words about mankind which bear repeating:

Our deepest fear is not that we are inadequate.

Our deepest fear is that we are powerful beyond measure.

It is our light, not our darkness that most frightens us.

We ask ourselves: who am I to be brilliant, gorgeous, talented and fabulous?

Actually, who are you not to be?

You are a child of God. Your playing small doesn't serve the world.

There's nothing enlightened about shrinking so that other people won't feel insecure around you.

We were born to make manifest the glory of God that is within us.

It's not just in some of us; It's in everyone.

And as we let our own light shine, we unconsciously give other people permission to do the same.

As we are liberated from our own fear, our presence automatically liberates others.

As Mandela said, every single person has the seeds of greatness within. In many cases, these seeds lie dormant, while the person struggles with the mundanities of life, believing that is all there is.

If only you could all see the brightness you carry within. For to focus on this is the key and the hope for your future on your planet.

If each of you reading this book were to expand your vision of yourself as a being, and act upon that expanded version, even in a minor way, a significant change would take place. Greatness can be infectious. You may have noticed that when you are generous towards someone, in most cases, that person feels like reciprocating. And if you are mean to someone, that is what you often receive in return. We are not suggesting you all attempt to become world leaders, but that in small ways you allow yourself to reach further towards the person you could be.

What is greatness in this context? We see greatness as:

- being open to others' opinions without preconceived judgement;

- being able to share of what you have, without fear of lack;

- being aware of and able to share your greater thoughts and truths, without fear of others' responses, but with compassion;

- being able to appreciate all that is offered to you – including sensory experiences, the presence of others, learning and diversity;

- the ability to recognise yourself as part of a greater whole, and act wisely and courageously upon this understanding;

- recognition and use of your particular talents; and

- the ability to act upon new information with flexibility and integrity.

If you were to choose one of these and focus on developing those qualities in your life, you would make a significant change.

Do you understand yet that in becoming a greater person, you are benefiting not only yourself, but all mankind, and even Earth? We feel the need to repeat this, as these concepts are so crucial and have been so long misunderstood by so many. To some of you readers, this information is not new. But perhaps an affirmation of your beliefs is useful right now. We hope so.

## Suffering and imbalance

It has long been held by many in your lands that to suffer is to die a little. We put it to you now that this is not so. Suffering is one of your human conditions without which you would not know joy. Honour your suffering, for it comes as a teacher and a torch to light up your happy times.

There is a further misunderstanding about suffering, at a deeper level in your world – one could say, in the psyche of mankind. This is a largely unconscious misunderstanding, but nevertheless extremely potent in its effect. Mankind holds that it is acceptable for some of its members to do the suffering for the good and balance of the greater whole. So, while millions starve, thousands live lives of luxury and squandering. While suffering *is* a necessary condition, it is neither necessary nor useful on this scale, and in this unbalanced way.

We are aware that for you to correct this imbalance would mean vast social and economic changes, which would conflict with the value systems of many at present. All we ask for the time being is that you become aware that this is not a workable system, and that suffering in moderation can benefit many people, but excessive suffering does more harm than good.

## Strengths and weakness

Another issue we wish to discuss is regarding man's notion of strength. In your world, strength has come to mean might or power, and there is the idea that might is right. This is confirmed by many of your political systems, by the concept of voting, the concept of war and in many sports. The natural corollary is that weakness is wrong.

Let us explore some other ideas about strength and weakness.

Imagine this scenario: Two footballers collide on the field. One becomes angry and hits the other, who refuses to be violent in return. Which one has shown weakness and which one strength?

And this: A couple are arguing about where to go on holiday. The woman really wants to go to the mountains, but realises when the man starts shouting how badly he wants to go to the beach. She decides to let him have his way and graciously ends the argument. Who is being strong here?

Try this one: Two politicians have both made mistakes in the past, which have disadvantaged certain sectors of the community. One apologises, while the other excuses himself, claiming it is the past and one must look to the future. Where is the strength and where the weakness?

Strength means following your convictions and values, until they are altered as a result of new

47

information. While weakness is following your immediate desires without regard for the other consequences.

Not all situations are as simple as those cited above. Take the example of two nations who disagree on the boundaries of their land. One instigates a war. What does the other do? Send off its fittest young to be killed? Capitulate and thereby compromise its people?

Over recent decades, your world has come a long way towards realising that there is might in discussion, negotiation and compromise. But there is still a long way to go.

## Leadership

A better system would be to appoint elders, chosen not for their political expertise, but rather for their wisdom, philanthropy, philosophy, fair-mindedness, impartiality and integrity. As long as you have divisions in your world – countries, states, communities – each group would appoint a council of elders, to preside over major decisions that have the potential to lead to conflict. An international body of elders, would draw up a world 'mission statement', which would be referred to in decision-making. Decisions would be made according to principles based on the long term consequences for the whole of mankind, rather than short term gains for a minority. Many tribal peoples lived peacefully in this way for centuries, until disturbed by the intrusive and competitive colonising nations.

There would still be legal systems, political systems,

law enforcement and so on, but major discussions and appointments would be weighted by the opinions of the elders, and in the case of possible conflict, they would have the final say. Voting would not be a relevant way of making decisions. Instead, representatives of differing points of view would discuss issues until resolution was reached.

## Acceptance and resistance

This is not the only way for you to achieve stability on Earth. It also depends on your ability to 'go with the flow'. What this often-used phrase really means is that you always have the choice of either moving with circumstances, towards their resolution, or moving against circumstances and away from resolution. This may sound ambiguous, so to clarify, here is a story:

A boy is getting on a bus, when a girl pushes in front of him. He can either insist on his right to be first; or he can make way and allow her to go first as she wishes. If he decides to do the former and pushes himself in front, he will be able to get into the bus first, but he would be subtly agreeing with the girl that there is a conflict between them. This conflict is then unresolved and needs to manifest again until resolution is reached. If the boy decides to bring the conflict out into the open and discuss the girl's behaviour with her and his rights, he would be giving much energy to the conflict and affirming its power. If he decides to let the girl complete her action, and to realign his actions to this new input, he would be 'going with the flow', and there would be no conflict and no carry-over into the future. Conflict must always have at least two sides.

For 'going with the flow' of this sort to work, it must be integrated at every level. If the boy is inwardly annoyed about the girl's behaviour but lets her go, he is still feeding a conflict.

Now you are probably thinking that this would not be appropriate in all situations. You are absolutely right. In a serious situation, say one of physical or mental abuse, to 'go with the flow' is not to allow the abuse to continue, but to go with the flow of what seems to be right according to natural laws. According to natural laws, man has free will, and man is naturally in a state of love. Therefore the abuser is breaking natural law by subjecting the abused to an unloving situation. The situation is unnatural and potentially damaging for both parties. To 'go with the flow' may be disastrous, but to go with the natural flow would ensure that the abuse stops. The abused would, in this case be upholding natural law by doing everything in his power to stop the abuse. This may mean fighting back, discussion, seeking help or running away. Ultimately, these actions will recreate a state of balance, both without and within. For, as you know, external events usually mirror internal reality. Thus the person who is abused by another is also abused by himself. In resisting the external abuser, the 'victim' is reasserting power over his own internal abuser, and balance is restored.

## Abuse, natural law and children

What of innocent children who are abused? How can they fight back to restore the balance? Here again is an exception. Rigid rules are a figment of man's imagination and of his hope for order and control over an unpredictable and unimaginably complex universe.

Children are a group of young people comprising many different beings. Remember that the future and the past are all happening now, at once – time being one of man's hopeful systems of control. Children in abusive situations are sometimes balancing out past or future events, and sometimes providing opportunities for others to learn about themselves. Children are your greatest teachers. They instruct without conscious awareness that this is their role. And they are also your quickest learners.

On a conscious level, adults believe their role is to teach children, who adopt the same belief. Therefore, too often what children learn is tainted by what adults believe they should learn. In your society, the notion has been developed that if a child does not behave according to the adult's rules, he is bad and should be punished. This belief exacerbates greatly any damage that abuse might do to a child. In the natural course of events, if a child were abused, he would realise that the abuser is the one behaving unnaturally. However, the child living with man's rules has come to believe that if he is abused it must be because he is bad. This, of course, can have tragic consequences, the main one being lack of self love, leading all too often to the belief that further punishment is in order. This is the beginning of the cycle of abuse.

The only way to stop this cycle once it has developed, is through the redevelopment of self love. The only way to prevent the cycle from occurring would be to dispel the myth of 'badness' and the need for punishment from your lives. It would be very difficult, well-nigh impossible for you to do this now, as you have such a well-developed system of crime and punishment. But it bears understanding. At least you could implement the theory in the raising of your children. There are no bad children; there are no bad things children do. Sometimes their actions cause you problems to be solved, but that is all. Therefore, your society would benefit by showing its children that they are completely loveable, and by helping them become aware of the consequences of actions in a clear, supportive manner.

## Indifference versus caring

The next point we would like to raise is one of indifference. Indifference is the pallor of your society. It is the ability you have developed to 'turn a blind eye' to your neighbour's distress. Your rationale is that you are too busy, too distressed yourself, or cannot help anyway. The effect of this indifference is that thousands, millions suffer needlessly, through lack of love. All you need to do to help is *care*. That does not mean worry, which is a destructive way of using energy. To care is to love and feel connected. This is energising for both parties and, in fact, creates positive change. Of course, to act upon your connection by helping in a tangible way is beneficial, but that is not the only way to make a difference.

What is the cause of all this suffering? It is mankind's global refusal to accept responsibility for being who he truly is. Suffering is caused by a lack of acceptance that you are really gods – perfect and magnificent just as you are. In some of your writings this problem is called separation from God. You have separated yourselves from your own perfection, and hence created suffering. You have also, out of your suffering, created greed in an attempt to assuage the separation and the emptiness that goes with it. In order to balance, globally, the greed which is indulged in by so many, others must suffer lack. So it follows that a way to reduce lack on your planet is to reduce greed. And the way to reduce suffering, lack and greed is to remember who you really are.

CHAPTER 4

# Ours is not to reason why, ours is but to live & die...

## Individual differences

Eventually it happens to everyone on your planet. There comes a time when you ask questions about life. Is there a God? What is my purpose? Who am I? Where am I going? Is there a life after death?

To some, these questions are all-important, and the perceived answers dictate the direction of your lives, and even your choice of friends. To others, they are overwhelming, an unnecessary burden in an already stressed life. They are forgotten or ignored in the hope that they will go away.

## Inward and outward pursuits

Neither one nor the other of these reactions is better. The reality is that different people have different priorities. There are those among you who scorn others not seen to be interested in 'spiritual' pursuits. What many do not recognise is that you all cannot fail to be 'spiritual'. You *are* spirits! However, focussing on your spiritual nature is often a distraction from the purpose of playing out your role in human form.

You have incarnated in order to experience, and thus to become aware. When you are too focussed on your discarnate qualities, you are 'missing the boat'. Your awareness will come from your earthly experiences, first and foremost. There is only a useful place for meditation and contemplation *in relation to* the outer human experience – day-to-day living. These tools are helpful in turning experience into awareness, but not in creating awareness alone. For human awareness to be meaningful it must relate to the human experience, which is one of form.

The person who is only outwardly focussed on his activities is lacking in the process of transforming them into awareness. Whereas the person who meditates many hours per day is lacking in the true experiential basis of his awareness. Between the two lies balance. Here is a state of incarnate wisdom, in which man can decipher his real purpose and needs.

## The need for purpose

It is very important to have a sense of purpose, even just for the next moment and even if the purpose may change frequently. Humans desperately need this sense of purpose, and if they do not find a meaningful one, they will invent another. This invention may be conscious or unconscious. This is another cause of your problems on Earth. There are so many who, through forgetting, are unable to contact their real sense of purpose. These rather lost souls ache until they find a goal of some sort. The goal may be one which benefits your society or, more often, one which benefits the individual's ego, such as power at work, more money, a bigger house, even an attractive partner. While these goals are held there is little chance of the individual finding his true purpose, as he is preoccupied and believes he knows the direction in which he is headed. The benefit of meditation is that it may allow man to release his hold on his material goals long enough to remember his spiritual ones. In other words, to by-pass the ego and hear the soul.

## Daily reflection (exercise)

Meditation does not have to be an emptying of the mind. It can be equally effective as a lateral shift of the mind. If each person were to set aside just 5 minutes at the end of the day to answer the following questions, your world would soon be a healthier place:

What did I do today that I am proud of?

What did I do today that I regret?

What have I learnt today about myself?

How do I want to be different tomorrow?

## Material and spiritual goals

Mankind has endless choice. Yet so many of you have chosen such limited and short-term goals. Most of these goals, in the long run, achieve so little for you, your loved ones and your planet. We fail to see the joy in material possessions, and we observe so many who have so much and are so unhappy.

We see others who are quite content with very little. This illustrates that materialism does not create happiness. Yet, on the whole, humankind is racing blindly, desperately towards material gains, with scant regard for the consequences.

We notice that those who are truly happy are those who have a purpose that benefits their own souls or mankind. The reason for their happiness is that they are in relationship with their souls. Let us imagine for a moment someone who is totally materialistic or hedonistic, someone for whom possessions or pleasures are of paramount importance. To this person, a day without pleasure or acquisition of some kind is a waste. This approach is not a recipe for joy.

Your progress is not a reflection of you alone. It is, in fact, a joint effort. You may not realise it, but you are affected by a myriad of influences, far beyond your understanding. These influences are subtle but powerful, and play a part in your decision-making. You still have the ultimate choice in your decisions, but your thoughts are often swayed, unbeknownst to you. The next part of this chapter will briefly examine some of these invisible influences.

## Invisible influences

To most of humankind, extraterrestrials are the stuff of science fiction and movies. But they are real – *we* are real. We have been around as long as you have, but many of us choose to be in a different dimension for our safety and for your peace of mind. Our mission here is to help you to adjust to your environment, and the forthcoming changes, and we do so in a gentle and sensitive manner. The main methods we have of influencing you are to show you through experience, and to provide you with mind pictures. We may feed your minds with information about objective reality, but we would never restrict your choices.

Some of you already know that there are others in the universe unlike us, who also seek to interact with you, and they certainly do. There are those amongst you who are not, in fact, 'earthlings', but who have come here from other places with the express purpose of learning about and from you. These beings do not always have your interests at heart. We do not condone their behaviour, but have little power over them, unfortunately. We tell you this in the hope that you will be empowered rather than frightened by this knowledge.

These beings have been with you for all time, influencing you and using you for their own ends. They try to learn about relationships, emotions and other matters from you, but do not have the intrinsic capability to put their findings to good use. Hence they still need you to study, in the hope that somehow they can blend with you and develop your abilities. We see that they will never be able to do this, but they will not believe that. Instead, they have been trying, quite successfully in many cases, to bring your vibrations in line with theirs, assuming their experiment will work better that way. It will not. However, in the process, mankind has been reduced, and because of this, has made many more unwise decisions than he otherwise would have. The explanation we gave earlier about your development and gradual desecration of Earth's patterns, does not contradict what we are telling you now. Mankind was, in a sense, unwittingly steered down a wrong course, by beings he did not know existed. This may sound far-fetched, but it is a truth we believe you now need to be aware of.

Much of the technology that is at the root of many of your problems did not come from Earth. It was passed on to you with the express purpose of taking you further from your destiny of greatness. This may puzzle you. Many of you may be thinking that your technologies have been a wonderful addition to life. However, the beings who sent them were well aware that you did not have the intellectual capacity to use them wisely, and that they would be your downfall. These beings hold man somewhat in awe, are jealous and would either like to be like you, or use you, which would ultimately destroy you. They are still hoping for the former.

We are pleased to be able to inform you that there are many other more benign influences which have helped to ensure your survival and relative safety. Angels do indeed exist.

## Discretion

Never in the history of mankind has he had as much help as is being offered now. It is coming from many different directions and many different kingdoms – as you would put it. It is imperative for man to become clear on which influences are helpful and which are rather manipulative. The way to tell is through your heart chakra. It will resonate with those on your side, but not with those who seek to use you. If you are not sure whether to listen to advice or information you are receiving, do the following: Relax, preferably lying flat on your back if possible and appropriate. Focus on your heart, breathing slowly and regularly. Become familiar with the feel of your heart. Then think of the information you are unsure of. If it is unsound, your heartbeat will tend to speed up. If it is sound, your heartbeat will feel the same, or become slower. Any signs of discomfort in your heart indicate an unsound idea.

## Time

Another tip you will need to successfully navigate through this time, is that of dealing with that very thing – time.

As we have already explained, time is only a human construct, but you do live within this construct, and therefore need ways of dealing with it. It is our observation that an increasing number of you are having difficulty with time. You feel unable to accomplish enough in the time you have. This is a fallacy and yet it is true. What is fallacious about it is that you are accomplishing more than ever before, but much of it is devoid of meaning for you. That is why it seems as though you are not doing enough. The trick is to cut out as much as possible that for you personally is not relevant or meaningful. That does not mean becoming selfish – it merely means becoming aware of the meaning in your life. So become clear on the purpose behind what you are doing, and if there is no relevant purpose, cut it out. This can make a surprising difference, not only to how much you achieve, but how you view your day.

Thirdly, we feel you need to be aware of the belief system you hold about money. If you believe it is the only way to get what you want, it will be. However, if you trust life to provide what you need, this will be done in surprising ways, and not always around money.

CHAPTER 5

# Now is the hour of our discontent.

## Waiting, uncertainty and confusion

On Earth, at present, there is much confusion. There is a sense of something impending. Many believe that rather dire events are soon to take place, and many fear a sort of 'pay back' by Earth for what humans have done to her. It is a time, in a sense, of waiting, and in that wait, as though before death, there is a mental reckoning taking place. On top of that, there are influences from outside on the collective human consciousness. These influences seek to speed up man's evolution, in order to assist a healing of the global and universal problems that have been created.

This state of waiting, and yet changing unconsciously and involuntarily, creates confusion and uncertainty in the human mind. This is why it is so important for you to learn to be flexible and live within the unknown. You need to adapt, rather than resist. If you resist, you cause pain and slow your process. If you gently accept the change you are in, it will be painless, and may indeed be joyful, as you discover realms you had not believed possible before.

## Embracing change with clarity

In order for you to understand some of the changes taking place, we would like to tell another short story:

Once, long ago, there was an old man who lived with his wife. Every day he would go to fetch water at the same place. One day his wife, who had been talking to friends, told him there was a well closer to their home, one that had even more water. But he refused to listen to her, as he was set in his ways. He continued to fetch water, day after day, at the further well. Every day he would leave at the same time as another old man, and return long after the other man had returned. After many weeks of this, the second man asked him why he did not accompany him to the closer well, and he replied 'But I have always gone to that well. Why should I change now?'

And the friend replied 'Perhaps it would be easier for you.' The old man still refused, and months later, his friend passed him again. 'Still using that old well are you?' the friend asked.

'Yes' said the old man 'and what's wrong with that?'

'Nothing' replied the friend, and went on his way.

The old man continued in this vein for many years until he did not have the energy to reach the further well, then he tried the closer one for the first time. It was much easier for him, and he silently wondered why he had not been there before.

Everyone needs to embrace change in their own time. You cannot make value judgements about who accepts change and who does not. It is a matter of personal readiness. Those who are ready earlier are ready earlier, and that is all one can deduce. Remember, there is a reason for all human decisions that is known only to the decision-maker, and sometimes not even by him.

Readiness depends on a few factors. Those who have accepted change before will be more likely to embrace change again. Those who have always struggled to maintain the status quo will struggle again.

This is no time to give up. It is also not the time to be daunted and to succumb powerlessly to changes. What we are suggesting to you who are ready to make change, is that you do it consciously, with clear understanding and intent.

This clarity might be difficult to attain in a situation of unchartered territory. We ask only that you set aside moments in which to gain clarity. This does not mean embarking on a rational thinking journey, but rather being open to insights which will be given to you.

## The power of mind and soul

You are fortunate to be alive at a wonderful stage of human evolution, one that could surpass your wildest imaginings in terms of human accomplishments. We are not referring to technology here, but to the power of the human mind and soul. When these are harnessed together, anything can be accomplished. It is when the mind is harnessed alone that it is a dangerous instrument. Our dear wish is that you will learn to combine the powers of these two amazing parts of yourselves to create a destiny beyond your present hopes, which would benefit us all and the whole of creation. If this sounds grand, it is.

## Drive, will, spirit and patience

We want you to realise that in order for you to succeed, you will need various attributes. The most important of these is will – the will to succeed. This comes from a human spirit that is well nourished. If your spirit is under-nourished, and therefore weak, you may succumb to difficulties and give in easily. The nourishment of the spirit is similar to that of the soul. The spirit needs to be heard, and to be respected. Therefore, listen to your spirit and that of others. If everyone's spirits were respected, there would be no need for war on your planet. Nourish each other by encouraging others to 'follow their star'. Never diminish others' dreams, for these are the staple food of the spirit.

The spirit also needs meaning. If it has to exist in an environment that is bereft of meaning, it withers. So seek meaning in your lives – any meaning will feed the spirit, but not necessarily the soul. The soul is only fed by meaning that relates to its progress.

Drive is the third attribute you will need to succeed. Drive is not the same as spirit, although it is created by spirit. Drive is the ability to go on when things get difficult; the ability to remain with eyes on the goal, while traversing a pebbly path. One can have spirit and not channel it into drive – instead it can get caught up in ego. Will is the dream or direction, spirit is the engine and drive is the fuel. If the engine has no fuel it gets nowhere. If the engine has fuel but no direction, it has nowhere to go

Apart from will, meaning and drive, on your exciting future journey you will need a great deal of patience towards circumstances, yourself and others. You may need the ability to wait for others to catch up or for others to understand. You may need patience with yourself and your own perceived unreadiness. Your own flaws will become more apparent to you and the temptation will be to judge yourself and others. You may feel as though you are champing at the bit for the next stage of your life when it is not yet forthcoming.

Teach others what you are learning. This will not only help them, but will also help us in our endeavours to recreate balance in your world. For there is so much knowledge held by so few of you, and such a strong need for it to be shared. It is never wasted when it is disseminated. Even if it is not the right time for an individual to consciously accept the information, it is stored in the unconscious and retrieved at a later time. While in the unconscious it subtly influences thought patterns, gradually laying the person open to conscious acceptance.

## The holistic organism

The main point to bear in mind is the Oneness of all life. This concept is difficult for many to grasp, but inherently underlies the order of all things, and all problems. Most problems are caused by the denial, or attempted denial, of this fact.

A common example is the tendency not to want to give, for fear of losing too much. This is always a fallacy, for giving of any sort always gives to the whole – that means everyone benefits by it, not just the obvious receiver. Another example is a political one. Take a country in which some are rich and some poor. It is common for the poor to envy the rich, and even to rob them. In so doing, they are robbing the whole, including themselves. They thereby rob themselves, mirroring the way the rich were exploiting them originally.

Everything ultimately functions as one great organism. If one part of the organism is robbed, that robbed energy affects the whole. The vibration of the whole is altered and impacts upon all parts of the whole. Everyone loses. But, you might say, on a material level, the robber still has his plunder. This is, in fact, a very short term gain, because soon the organism, out of balance, must right itself. He who gained in one way, loses in another. You have repeatedly seen in many countries the toppling of wealthy magnates, subsequently being charged with fraud and losing their gains. The organism is always ultimately self regulating – sooner or later.

## Light and dark

However there is another principle at work – light attracts light, and dark attracts dark. The more light there is at any time within the organism, the more light will be formed by it, and vice versa. This means that any action which produces light has a double affect, on everyone. And any dark action has a doubly dark effect. The only way in which the light/dark balance is influenced is by man. The reason for this is that he has been given free will, and in order for it to be truly free, it must have an unimpeded consequence. So this is an area in which the organism is most at the mercy of man's thoughts and actions. The organism can regulate within the amount of light and dark it is given at any one time, but, apart from magnifying the ratio, it cannot change the condition. This is one of the dangers of the present time, to all of us. There is much light being produced on Earth, but a far greater amount of darkness, and this is affecting the whole organism, of which we are a part.

This is why we are so determined to help create more light on your planet.

The irony is that it would be so easy to reverse this problem, and the reversal would have such wonderful and wide-reaching effects. The chasm between the problem and the reversal is made of unawareness. If all people could truly see the whole situation as it really is, they would instantly change. However, the creation of awareness, or lifting of consciousness, is a slow process.

CHAPTER 6

# To be or not to be. That is the question.

## Money as a god

Do not risk sacrificing your world to the god, Money. It may be too late to reverse some things, but it is not too late to change the trend of materialism, in your Western world particularly. This is the time to address this pattern.

You will find in your political systems a hankering by many individuals for continued personal and political power. Occasionally, this drive is ideologically based, but more often it is founded on fear – fear of not being able to get, have, express or do as much as when in power.

## Fear and love

Yes, your world politics is basically run on fear. Fear that other countries or peoples will take over or spoil your country; fear that other groups will have more of what they want than your own group will; fear that change may disturb the status quo and the balance of power.

Imagine, for a moment, a world system based on love. This would mean looking at genuine human needs, rather than economic checks and balances. It would mean taking some excess from the rich, and distributing it to the poor. It would mean developing industries which support man and the Earth he lives upon, rather than those which destroy or abuse. For instance, fossil fuels, pesticides, weapons, violent games, and poisonous foodstuffs would be replaced with solar power, biodynamic farming methods, healing courses and tools, video games which would stretch the imagination in constructive directions, and healthy, chemical-free foods. Instead of spending billions of your dollars on space exploration, you would be looking to solve the problems at home first. You are trying to run before you can walk. Everything that you need to sustain you ALL is on your planet.

It is typical of man that he looks outside himself for a solution to his problems – on every level. On a global level, you are far more likely to spread your problems to other parts of the solar system than you are to solve them, unless you stay at home and make some changes.

We know that some of you are contemplating changes in the area of fossil fuel usage. This change will not be substantiated, unless there is a radical shift of consciousness among heads of government and industry.

We find it sad that such a beautiful, bountiful planet is being so mismanaged. However we realise that you are doing your best within the collective awareness you have. You need to realise that too, and have patience with yourselves. For constructive change will not be born of impatience or anger.

Your economies will soon flounder, giving you the opportunity to examine values other than monetary ones. Within the present economies of your world, there is not enough incentive to do this. Hence, you will create your own 'economic disaster', which would be more accurately termed 'therapy'. So when this happens, look upon it positively, for it is a good sign – a sign that balance may soon be regained.

Another occurrence to warn you about is the forthcoming climatic changes. This too, no matter how dire the scientists' forecasts, will be a regulator. It will change your food production patterns, ultimately to more suitable and sustainable ones. It will force man to evaluate his treatment of his host (the Earth), and to make some sensible decisions at the eleventh hour. It is true that more desert will eventuate, but desert, too, has a role that has not yet been understood. The desert is a very still place, where little happens. It is needed to counteract the busy-ness of mans' cities and inhabited areas. The Earth is an organism which operates on a system of balance. So the more active man becomes, the more deserts are needed.

Do not worry about overpopulation. Ultimately, that will take care of itself – it always does. That is again part of the balance. Use birth control by all means, but do not focus on possible overpopulation in the future. You have enough to focus on in the present. Your main aims should be to ensure that every person has enough to eat and drink, enough warmth and enough love. We assure you, again, that in your world there is enough of all these things for everyone. It is purely a question of distribution.

Would it surprise you if we were to tell you that many of your problems are caused by your possessions? Imagine, for a moment, hurling all sorts of goods off the face of the earth – into space if you like. There go toys, televisions, fluffy slippers, jewellery, cameras, carpets and garden statues flying off into the distance.

How would life be without them?

There would be less to maintain, less to guard, less to compare, less to desire. Instead, there would be more creativity, more physical work, more simple pleasures.

## The obsession with materialism

We are not suggesting you return to the dark ages; merely that you stop to consider the effect of technology and material possessions on your lives. Much of your stress is, in fact caused by your possessions and your perceived need for them. If they were not in existence, you would be more resourceful, more creative, more appreciative. You would not be attempting to fit so much into a day. Instead, you would focus more on the present – what you were doing right now.

There can be no turning back of the clock, nor should there be, but we ask you to ponder on the merits of having so many goods. For many, they act as millstones around the neck, preventing real progress. Remember, too, that as long as you have too much, others must suffer not having enough. That is how the balance is kept.

It would be wise to begin to discriminate carefully before buying more goods. Ask yourself if you really need them, or if they are just another outward sign of the materialistic age. If you honestly examine your motives for buying, you may often find them to be the following:

- others have it, so you must also

- it would make life easier

- it would give a good impression to others

- it would make you feel better (temporarily)

- it would be a way to spend your money

- it would distract you

- it would be fun (short term)

- it would fit the current (short term) fashion

- you feel pressured into buying.

None of these are really sound reasons for investing your space, time and money. There are more efficient ways to deal with the issues mentioned above. For example, to help a person in need can be distracting, fun, rewarding and make life easier for someone else.

Despite your considerable intelligence, you have allowed yourselves to become narrow in your problem-solving approaches. You have allowed your own stream of materialism to become a raging river, carrying you along at a rate you no longer understand or control. You have begun to interpret your problems in terms of the material, and their solutions in the same way.

## Being, having and doing

Now, you do live in a material world, this is true. But have you forgotten that your essence is spiritual? You are spiritual beings in a material playground. Your own BEING is the most relevant part of this scenario. Somewhere along the time line you have created, you have subjugated your being to your having and your doing. Please remember, these are only bitparts, not the main protagonists of the play. Your original task was to BE, and to support your being with the wonderful ability of doing. In order to do more widely, you discovered it helped to have. Having came third. Now everything has transposed, and we find that on Earth, for many of you, having is all important, followed by doing. Being is unvalued.

Being is your core. This is the quiet centre which accesses all knowledge, and is there to guide you in your thoughts and actions. If you lose sight of this powerful core, you will be more easily influenced by forces of which you may be unaware. Your inner centre is your connection point to all that is – the ultimate creative force. Without this you would be empty shells, rudderless boats – an open invitation for other forces to take over.

Please reconnect with your core selves, in any way you choose. There are now many teachers and resources to help you do this. Your own desire and intent is a strong factor by itself. If you truly want to make connection, and ask, it will happen. There has actually never really been a disconnection. You are always the being that you are. However you are not necessarily consciously aware of this, and therein lies the danger. The risk is in drifting along unawares. When this is the case, there is no force for change, and the prevailing trend gradually strengthens.

Ask yourself: *Who am I?...* Are you really the mother, the friend the healer, the lawyer, the potter... or is there something more to you, which you are ignoring? Something which ties the whole lot together, which directs the show, which provides the energy for the production?

Many people have a vague feeling that there may be something more, and that notion provides so much disquiet, because it is out of step with their lifestyles, that they keep busy enough to banish such thoughts. These people are depriving themselves of peace of mind. In effect, they have sentenced themselves to a life of hard labour, in order to avoid a truth which is far more gentle and enjoyable.

Much of the human race has become obsessed with accumulating tonnes of flour, when the project was to bake a cake.

The trick to combining being, doing and having, is to remember at all times that order of importance. Your having is to help you do and be, and your doing is to experience your being. Doing – interacting with the material world – is the way you experience your humanity. If you did not do, you might as well still just be in spirit form. The experience of interacting with the material form of your beautiful world is the gift you were given. You will never have another birthday present like it! So make the most of it, without forgetting who you are: the experiencer. In

English grammar you learn that there is a subject and an object in a sentence. It would not be a sentence without the subject. Do you see the parallel?

In conclusion to this point, we would like you also to recognise the great efforts that many of you have made in recent years. Many thousands of you have been teachers or pupils of the reconnection process, helping in each of your ways to change this trend, and gaining much personal satisfaction along the way. We thank you and urge you to continue in what you are achieving. It has made a difference globally, and will continue to do so – more so as momentum builds up. To those of you who are beginners on this path, we congratulate you for making yourselves available to read this book. This in itself indicates open-mindedness and the willingness to look further. We wish you much joy on your journey.

CHAPTER 7

# Listen… do you want to hear a secret?

## Handling new information

At this time in your evolution, there is much new information being given to you. This may be confusing, as some of it contradicts what you have been taught over many years.

We see that you are responding in a variety of ways. Some of you are not willing to entertain any notions contrary to those of the status quo, and will do whatever you consider necessary to quash the information, so that it is no longer a force to be reckoned with. Ridicule, abuse, threats, authoritarianism and even violence are used to silence bearers of information. Some are also threatened or frightened but are able to allow others to proceed in peace, merely avoiding contact themselves. Others are cautiously open-minded, listening and carefully evaluating the validity of what they are told. Still another group is excited by what they see as a form of salvation from man's ills, and is prepared to take on board even the most outlandish ideas, without due discrimination.

We suggest that at this time, you follow the open but cautious path. There is much information being passed on to you from many sources. Some of these sources are more reputable than others, and some are more genuine in their concern for you than others. So, as discussed in earlier chapters, listen to your heart before adopting new information as the truth.

One of these so-called truths is regarding 'mateship'. It has been told to some of you that your real home is elsewhere, and that UFOs will come and take you 'home'. We urge you to be very careful about this one, or you could be taken to someone else's home and for their purposes. There are a great number of different types of beings out there, with different levels of consciousness and motivation. Many of them do not have your interests at heart. There are indeed some 'in the wings' waiting for the time when you will be foolish enough to go with them voluntarily to places far less pleasant than your Earth. Remember, advanced technology does not necessarily mean advanced soul. It is true that there are others who are willing to rescue a number of you should the need arise, however, our hope is that you will be able to take care of yourselves and will not need our intervention. Hence books such as this, to help guide you along your way.

You are hearing many confusingly contradictory versions of the truth about your origins and your future. Let us just say that many of them are correct. The future has many versions of possibility at present, as it always does. It is up to you to collectively pick a version that suits you, and thus make it happen. The past is, in a sense, irrelevant to the future, in that the future can be based on not only the past that was chosen, but the other possibilities which were not. Therefore, it is not worth your while building up a picture of the past in order to construct a likely future from it. Instead, look at what you need, in a deep and collective sense, and build a future which will fulfil those needs. We are tempted to put in our penny's worth and say that it appears as though your needs in the future will revolve more around having a clean and living, beautiful world to play on, than about weapons, deodorants and big houses.

## Overcoming space-time barriers

Other secrets that are confusing you at present are to do with time and space. What we want you to understand here is that time and space are two dimensions of the same thing – your reality. Neither really exists in the absolute. This is why the laws of time and space are so often broken, causing much incredulity and wonder. If you connect to the absolute, or pass into a connection point, these concepts can, temporarily or permanently, cease to exist for you. It is possible for you to be in more than one place or time at once.

Few people have mastered this ability to transcend man's boundaries, and this is just as well, because most of humankind is not yet prepared for such perceived anomalies. Man still largely needs the restrictions of time and space in order to function effectively. This is slowly changing, and the need is growing for man to transcend his time/space barriers fairly soon. This is why there has been such an explosion of 'parapsychic' phenomena in recent decades, such a resurgence of interest in 'past lives' and in space travel.

Please realise that there are no barriers anywhere at all in reality. You are capable of anything, anywhere, any time. This is because you are what you call God. You are the divine, with a body wrapped around it, which you are still learning to drive. When you finally have your driver's licence, you will find yourselves able to do what only very few can do now. You will then be able to interact with your Earth without robbing her, for you will have no need for the pleasures you have sought for comfort in the past. You will be able to invent what you need, without the need for raw materials. The few who can do this now are here to show you what is possible.

However, until your consciousness has evolved further, you will not be ready for this power. If you were to develop these powers before you were ready, you could destroy all that you hold dear. They would be a threat similar to the nuclear one, but worse. So spiritual development has to precede inter-dimensional abilities. Those who find ways of cheating this system will be doing so at their peril. Many of you may have experienced glimpses of what you are capable of. You will be given opportunities as soon as you are ready, and do not need to consciously ask.

Time travel is not to be tampered with. To most of you at this stage it is a dangerous realm. To invite you to experiment with time travel would be similar to asking a four-year-old to conduct chemistry experiments unsupervised. If you are fascinated by the idea, read about it by all means, discuss it, but do not yet try it. You might succeed and you might not know how to get back. All sorts of chaos could be caused. Remember, when you are ready for it, it will happen to you, because it is an evolutionary stage.

An idea that probably also fascinates you, is the one about time warps. This, too, is a reality – one that your world as yet has little comprehension of. However, one of the by-products of space exploration is some discovery on the workings of time. It seems to you that even in a grain of sand, a myriad of tiny atomic structures exist in perfect symmetry and balance. Well, imagine how symmetrical and balanced the whole universe is, when compared to one grain of sand. It is no more and no less. Just as one minute is no more or less than one century. They are both time, and time is immeasurable in reality.

## Time warps and telekinesis

This may be difficult for you to grasp. Let us put it to you like this: in an hour there are 60 minutes; in a minute there are 60 seconds; in a second there are 100 milliseconds; in a year there are 365 days; in a decade there are 10 years, in a lifetime there may be 85 years. How long in a moment, in the present? It is all the present. The present makes a fool out of the whole time measurement system, for there is no beginning and no end to the present moment, nor is there any other moment. You have turned the moment into a cake and cut it into slices, giving each a name, but it is still a cake and all of its slices are there. Now, imagine someone takes a slice and eats it. What happens to the cake? It is still there. Part of it has moved and been transformed, but it is still a cake. The cake as a whole still exists, even if part of it has been changed. From the outside, we might come in and see an incomplete cake, and interpret it as a number of slices of cake, rather than one cake. From the inside, if we could imagine the cake was some kind of living organism we would feel an organism that had been divided into many smaller organisms. Each of these now becomes a separate unit, apart from the whole.

This is exactly how time warps occur. Man has powerfully divided the whole of time into chunks, which then take on an existence of their own, and which become separate from the whole continuum of time. Occasionally, someone trips into one of these chunks of detached time and gets stuck there for a while. It is not easy to reconnect with the main body of time from such a position, but when this is achieved, the individual finds that time has either not passed at all 'back home' on the continuum, or that a remarkable amount of time has passed. Time warps are a by-product of man's way of dealing with space time.

Another notion which is baffling some of you is that of telekinesis – the projection of objects through space by the power of the mind. This should not surprise any of the neurologists among you, dear readers! How do you project yourselves through space? Your mind makes a suggestion to your nervous system, which relays the message to your muscles, which act to produce movement. It is the mind which instigates the motion. The principles of telekinesis are identical.

Thought triggers electromagnetic response, which triggers the movement of matter.

The Earth and all on it have electromagnetic fields of one sort or another. Much information is carried by these fields. They are nature's telephones, one could say. When powerful messages are sent on these fields, they will override the less powerful messages. Let us imagine that the result of the usual messages is the effect of gravity. If an individual were able to counteract that instruction strongly enough, the effect of gravity would no longer hold sway, and the object would lift. If the message to go right or left or down were super-imposed, the object would follow. In a sense, natural laws are much simpler than you think. It is largely your need to analyse and explain according to your narrow scientific principles, which has complicated your understanding. Your science only takes into account what it already knows, thus limiting its horizons. There is so much you are now ready to understand, if you would accept a broader paradigm.

Before we venture further into realms more unknown to you, let us say this: you are now certainly entering a time of wonder and excitement; a time for discovering and rediscovering; a time for sharing of insights and for exploring your powers; for rejoining with the infinite and unfolding your potential. But with every light there is a shadow, and this stage is no exception. You will need to be very careful, as different individuals are at different stages of readiness, and there could be much unrest, and many trials for those willing to move forward. May we suggest that you not burst with missionary zeal to share your newfound knowledge with others who may not want it. Put out your knowledge in such a way that those who are ready will find it. There is no point in fighting a river – it will continue to flow, and you may be drowned in the process.

So be perceptive with others and understand where they are at. We would also like to suggest that you support each other through times of change. You will need like-minded souls around you, and would do well to seek them out. There are more of them around than many of you know. Find them at workshops, talks and group gatherings, and maintain contact, for you will need it.

Now, onto perhaps more extraordinary matters. There is a global, conscious knowing that times are changing too quickly and in dangerous directions on your planet, and that peace may not last long at a global level. The health of the planet and all on it is at risk. What we say to you is that none of this need count in your future, if you strongly do not wish it to. You have the potential to change your reality almost overnight. There are many of you who are aware, and there are many of us willing to help. We are here, waiting for the invitation. We will come at any time the signal is given, as long as our safety is ensured and we will be greeted in peace. Know that you are only a threat to us in that we would not wish to have to harm any of you in our defence. Together we could turn your world into whatever you truly desire it to be, provided enough of you are willing to work with us. Until we are given the invitation by a significant representation of your people, we will not intervene at other than a consciousness level, unless there is an urgent need. We respect your free will. However, we must also respect the needs and wishes of the rest of creation, and we would not see your actions jeopardise others.

We would like to assure you that we share a deep desire to help you, and that we are willing at any time. Please consider our offer.

## We are here to help

In the meantime, those individuals who would like our help only have to ask, in order to receive telepathic help. We are able to communicate with you in this way – this is how this book is being written. However, we would not intrude uninvited in such a specific manner. If you ask us to communicate out of curiosity we will not, but if your motives are constructive we will assist, and will be able to offer input to you on many issues. Be clear on who you are inviting, if you do ask for help. We are beings of light from the Pleiades, originally from Orion. If you receive a response to your request for communication, check that it is indeed us. Just ask, and listen for an answer.

What you will find, if you do make contact with us, is that we will be able to give you a different insight into many of your concerns, and broaden your understanding and perceptions.

Another point for you to be aware of is that there is no real barrier between us. We exist in a different dimension and can be wherever we want to be at any time. In other words, we can do what you will soon learn to do. We can also link our consciousness with yours, so that we can be there instantaneously if you ask for us. (Many other beings can do these things too, but are less evolved than man on a soul level.) We look forward to more conscious contact with you and to being of service to you.

It may be hard for you to understand that we do not come in fear but from the spirit of love. There is nothing you could do that we could not undo before the act, if we really wanted. However, our prime task is to honour your free will – that was the experiment. Consider us as your brothers and sisters. We are all of one family originally, and we love you. The fact that most of you are not yet clear about our existence, does not alter this. We see you, even if you do not see us, and we care about what we see. We are here to help and are pleased that you recognise us more than before. However, we are not offended if you choose to believe we do not exist. This is your prerogative.

CHAPTER 8

# Now is the only moment.

## Being in the present

We have discussed time in various ways, but we have not yet explored the value of the present moment. If you were able to learn to be fully in the present time, you would be able to do things most of you only dream of. This would mean you would be able to have full access to your intellect and abilities.

For most of you, it would be an achievement to stay focussed on the moment for even a minute of your time. For you allow yourselves to be distracted by fears regarding the past and future for most of your waking time. This has been very limiting for you, allowing you to realise only a small percentage of your capabilities.

It seems to us that you would be able to achieve so much in your world if you were able to be just a little more in the present. Imagine a home being run by someone who is out most of the time – this is rather like your situation on Earth. The problem is that it is unconscious. If you chose consciously to revisit the past for a reason, that would be different. But instead, what happens is that you drift willy-nilly from future to past to present, not fully attending to any of them. In full consciousness, progress can be accelerated.

It seems rather as though you were not concerned enough about what is around you to fully attend to it. And yet that is not the case at all. It is because you are so concerned that you seek help from the past and future. You call upon your past experiences, your past fears and disappointments, hurts and grievances, and steer yourselves forward upon their memories. You whizz to the future to determine what might go wrong, who might disapprove, and you surf forward on this risk assessment. You often do not even see how out of line the present is with the past or with your perception of the future. In so doing you are not responding to the real situation, but to a conglomerate of fears and doubts of your own making. Thus you miss many opportunities to make a change and to have an effect. Particularly now, your reality is changing so fast, that to react to the present from the perception of the past is possibly dangerous, and certainly a waste of opportunity.

This is the only moment in which you can express who you are. This is the only moment in which you can be free. This is the only moment in which you can make a difference. This is the only moment in which you can feel love.

## Judgement versus joy

Untie yourselves, dear friends, from the shackles of time that bind you and be free to be in the moment. The moment is made of joy – it is only your experiences and interpretations that tell you otherwise. They lead you to the other j word: judgement. Remove the fear, anger and other unhappy emotions from any experience and it can be one of bliss, of fully being alive, no matter what it contains. E-motion moves us away from ourselves, whereas love takes us towards our core, where bliss resides.

You have been gifted with the ability to experience emotion. This adds to the richness and diversity of your experience, but it can also reduce your experience if not kept in perspective. One of your tasks has been to learn how to deal with emotions. It is one that has had you confused for centuries. At times, you have believed that emotions are reflections of the truth. This is rarely so. They are usually nothing more than impulsive physiological responses to thoughts. At other times you have believed that they are wrong and a sign of weakness. This is no closer to the truth. Emotions are like the spice on your dinner. They add flavour to your lives. However, they are to be regarded with caution in terms of how they affect your actions. Experience your emotions – that is what they are there for. Be responsible for them as your emotions. Let others know you have them if you like, but do not blame others for them. They are only yours after all. Once you have felt them, let them go before you decide on a course of action.

Do not let your emotions dictate your behaviour, or you will be giving away your free will. Your emotions are largely dictated by your past experiences, so reacting to them is being led by the past, instead of being in the present.

Some would say it is best to 'go by your feelings'

in a situation. They are speaking of intuition, not emotion. Intuition takes you inwards, to where your higher self is. It puts you in touch with knowledge otherwise inaccessible to you, so that you can make wise decisions. Intuition requires listening. Emotion asks for shouting, crying, running away, hugging or some other outward display. That is how you can tell the difference.

## Emotions versus intuition and love

Sometimes emotion is mistakenly called love. Approval, pleasure, pride, sexual arousal and neediness are not the same as love. Love is different from emotion. It is a state of energy – a particular vibration which tunes into much of creation. It is the same as at-one-ment or universal consciousness, or enlightenment. Love joins, emotion separates.

We ask you not so much to be aware of your emotions, as to be aware of your responses to them. Do not let them rule you and remove your powers of discretion, for they can be tricksters, based as they so often are on misinformation. We suggest you regard your emotions with tolerant amusement, as you might regard a hysterical younger brother. They are to be enjoyed and not taken too seriously.

The present is a gift like no other. It is the only one that allows you to be and to act. Use it fully, and you will be amazed at the freedom you enjoy.

Many of you will not know how to start being in the present. Here is a little exercise for you to try:

# THE 'NOW' EXERCISE

---

*Close your eyes and breathe deeply...... in......*
*and out......*
*in...... and out......*
*Slowly let your thoughts about other times drift away*
*and begin to focus on NOW......*
*how does the present feel......*
*smells......*
*temperature......*
*movement......*
*sounds......*
*what else can you sense?*
*How is your body right now?......*
*where does it feel light?......*
*where does it feel heavy?......*
*does it feel supple?......*
*does it feel stiff?......*
*how is your breathing?......*
*relaxed?......*
*tense?......*
*where is there pressure against your body?......*
*what are your thoughts......*
*send them off again and focus on your senses......*
*If you were to respond to the present situation, what*
*might you do......*
*respond in some small way......*
*Having changed something about the present, you*
*have now created a new present......*
*Notice again how your senses are perceiving this*
*moment......*
*smells...... sounds......*

*touch......*
*pressure......*
*and how your thoughts may be taking you away......*
*Bring yourself back to the senses......*
*see how long you are able to purely experience this*
*moment......*

———————————

You probably found yourself not just being aware, but quickly starting to judge. Not cold, but *too* cold, not tense but *wrongly* tense.

## Judgement versus discrimination

This kind of judging distorts perception only too frequently. It causes you to block out certain parts of your reality, and highlight others. This is premature judgement, or judgement based on the past. It is different from discrimination – a useful tool which for you in the coming times will be imperative. Discrimination comes from deep within. It is a function of the oversoul, the higher self, and may be supported by the mind, but is often distracted and diverted by it. When you want to discriminate between courses of action, focus on each possibility in turn, and carefully note your response. As we have said in earlier chapters, if your heart rate slows, the action is in tune with your soul, if it speeds up it is causing soul stress.

## Soul needs and addictions

Until you learn to discriminate in this way, life will be unnecessarily difficult for many of you, with many of your decisions going 'against your grain'. You will no doubt be basing most of your decisions on desire, rather than on inner needs. When the desire and inner soul needs are at loggerheads, there is always pain. The way to ease the pain is to start following your soul needs. They lead to joy, whereas desire leads only too often to addiction. Thus in your societies many have trouble with addictions to drugs, food, status, gambling, luxury, ease, socialising, analysing, preaching, crime, anger, sex, relationships, power, fame, attention, approval, security, excitement, entertainment and many other pursuits, traits and objects.

Any addiction causes a reduction in freedom and is therefore limiting. So if you want to realise your true potential as beings, it is time you stopped and looked carefully at your addictions, and did some discarding of desires. If you gently push your desires out of the way, your soul needs can become more apparent to you. You will be able to hear the little voice that was there all along. It was drowned out before by the strident whining of your desires!

There is another way of being. In our own societies we do not compete to get our needs satisfied. We work together for the good of the whole, and in so doing our needs are realised. We also play a great deal. Play to us is pure experience – tuning fully in to life and the moment. Whenever we have important business to complete, we give a percentage of the time over to play. This helps us focus more effectively and enjoy our tasks more fully. There is never a moment that we are not aware of, thus we can respond so much more effectively. We never had the distraction of emotions as you did. We have a capacity for love which is more or less unparalleled in your world, but our emotional range is limited. This is neither good nor bad. It just is.

Still on the topic of the moment, we notice that to many of you there seem to be fewer moments in the day than there used to be! This of course is not really so – the moment is a never-ending continuum as it always was. But your relationship to your time is changing. As you collectively change in density, for that is what is happening, you are moving at a different rate in relationship to space, and it seems to you as though time is speeding up. There is a message in this too, which some of you have read: that you are trying to do too much. It is a kind of enforced 'go slow' for you, as you realise you cannot do as much as you used to. If you are fully aware of the moment, you will be satisfied with whatever you do manage to achieve, and more realistic in setting your goals.

We believe there is a need for clarification here. Being aware of the moment does not mean wafting about in purple clothing, meditating and avoiding decision-making. Far from it. It means being an active part of life, setting goals, deciding and acting from a place of awareness, rather than from a place of fear or unconsciousness.

## The future is changeable

It is not until you are aware of the future that you will be able to do something constructive about it. You can only know the future when it has manifested into the present. Until then, it only exists as a myriad of possibilities. The future is an area about which you at this stage know very little, even though it is uppermost in your concerns. So it would be correct to say 'look after the present and the future will look after itself'. You would find that if you were to do this, more favourable futures would be created very quickly.

Our purpose with this book is to give you a glimpse of how your world appears to us, and how you could help yourselves to form a happier future than the one you are now creating. We certainly do not wish to see you hurt or hurting others. This is why we are concerned. It is our belief, from what we see and know, that you will change direction, given the right amount and quality of information. This is why so many of us are helping you. If we thought it was too late, we would not be communicating with you in this way. It is not too late for you to change to new paradigms – of faith and hope, instead of fear and greed.

## Creating reality

Please believe us that you do create your reality. This is a part of the system of free will. You make the choices and you bear the consequences. The choices do eventuate in one form or another. This is a concept many of you still do not understand. Your thoughts of the present create your future. This is absolutely – not partly or symbolically – true. Every thought you have is a powerful impulse steering reality one way or another. We wonder, if you really understood this, how your thinking would change!

Remember, if you will, the times when you sweated

over an assignment, and at the completion of it were disappointed. It was not as good as you had hoped it would be. It is at these times that you may have thought 'I'm really not much good at...'. This thinking would have led to a gradual decline not only in your ability, but in your confidence and love for yourself. Without sufficient love for yourself, you would not be able to do many things which otherwise would have been easy for you. This is one of the ways you have diminished yourselves. If, on the other hand, you had, on completion, thought, 'I could do even better next time', you would have achieved a very different result. You would be reminding yourself of your infinite capacity, and this would encourage you to greater success and self-love.

## Self love

Before we go any further, there is another concept to clarify. Some of you still cling to the notion that self love is 'bad', equal to ego obsession and conceit. This is not so at all. In fact, false modesty is closer to ego than self-love is. To love yourself is to appreciate the amazing being that you are. You have not created this being. You have, in a sense, rented the space, and are making a better or worse job of looking after it. We are here using 'you' to mean your personality, the outer 'you', the 'you' that others identify. To be modest about something that you have not created smacks of false ownership and ego identification.

To love yourself is to love God, whether or not you subscribe to man's conventional set of religions. If you compare the human race to a fleet of cars, it is as though you have become so taken with the fancy bodywork, that you have forgotten it is the engine that makes it go at all. Were it not for the engine, hidden behind the scenes, the car would be merely a useless decoration. Thus it is with the spirit and the body-personality. The outer, whether physically or psychologically, is merely a vehicle for the spirit. To totally identify with the outer is therefore to lose direction. Remember this.

CHAPTER 9

# Dearly beloved...

## Love, the vibration of unity

In this chapter we seek to enlighten you on a number of issues pertaining to love and relating with each other.

Firstly, do you realise that it is years in your time since many of you made love?

Your notions of sex and love have become intertwined in a most confused way. It is no wonder so many are craving sex, when what they really want is love. It has become unfashionable in your world to display genuine love – the bonding of two souls at a deep level, not necessarily accompanied by physical closeness. Love has nothing to do with gender or sexual preferences. It has everything to do with soul. Love springs from a genuine recognition of the Other – that means of the God in the other person, and of your own connection with that. Most of what you now call love is actually desire, need fulfilment and other forms of fear-based manipulation.

The patterns which you now find yourselves in have formed insidiously, and have been reinforced over many generations and cultures. The whole process is understandable, and we in no way wish you to blame yourselves any more than we would blame you. Please accept any new insights we might be giving you with a sense of discovery and excitement, rather than dismay. Having new understanding facilitates the making of changes.

We would ask you to write down who you really love, as opposed to who you believe you need, want or 'should' love. Some of you will find to your surprise that the page remains blank, others will be able to name several, and very few might be able to honestly have a non-exclusive number.

Forget for the time being, that you are in a solid, vulnerable body. Imagine yourselves to be pure spirit, which is what you are really. What would the world be like? There would be no untruths, for you would know instantly. There would be no sex as you know it, as there would be no bodies. There would be no jealousy about possessions and looks, for there would be no need for either. What would be left? Pure sparks of interaction between divine beings of light. There would be no complications to dull their brightness, and they would be fully aware of their beauty and completeness. They would also be fully aware of their connection, for there would be no complicating personalities, comparisons and other outward trappings to give them cause for division. These beings would be like leaves on the same stem, linked to the same source and co-existing without competition. They would be in harmony with their source and with each other. Each interaction would be a mini-replica of an interaction with the source – a flash of unity. In a sense, an interaction can be seen as closing a circuit between the source and two or more beings. When this takes place, a flash of love energy passes between those involved. Love energy is source energy. It is the basic stuff of all matter. Take all the love out of your world and nothing would hold together. We mean literally. Love is the vibration of unity.

It is time for you all to start feeling love again. This is imperative for your survival as a species. You will find that once you understand more clearly what love is, it will be easier to link into it. You have become confused and followed commercial, psychological and other ideas of what love is. It is now time to question all of those and ask for the genuine article.

## Sex, hurt, connection

Sex, as you know, is not love. Though it has become a rather risky pursuit, it has been considered safer by most of you, than love. Many of your songs refer to the trials and tribulations of love – the risks and the hurts. This is not love. It is personal involvement, and often dependence. Real love does not, cannot cause hurt, as there is no expectation. It is rather an openness to a pure connection. As such, it is extremely joyous, and this is where the confusion has crept in. Sex is, on a physical level, a connection, and is often most enjoyable. It is the closest you can get to the kind of connection and joy you reach through love, but is a weak version, we assure you.

Why did man lose much of his ability or desire to love? It was a gradual change, which paralleled his disconnecting from the Earth. As soon as he began to feel himself as a separate identity, he believed he should be able to 'go it alone', through mastering the Earth, instead of working co-operatively. His ego started to take over, creating competition and separation from himself, his fellows and his creator.

It has been both a sad and a joyous process to observe. In 'going it alone', man has made many destructive decisions, and has suffered, but he has also enjoyed a huge range of experiences, discoveries and developments. So it is by no means all problematic. It would be truer to say that it is cyclical, and the cycle has almost turned fully, necessitating a new phase.

So what we suggest is that you try to see each other in a new light – as beings rather than bodies. For that is what you are. See the bodies as a disguise if you like, for that is how you often use them. Realise the God in each of you and make a connection with that part when you interact. You will find relating to be not only much more satisfying, but much more efficient, as fewer games need be played out. The reason so many people play games on various levels is for recognition. When there is little love, there is little recognition. You are not seeing each other. You are looking past each other at your own desires, at the future or your activities. People starve spiritually in the absence of connection. To recognise another being is to help heal him. All it takes is eye contact, openness, and an awareness of his divinity (even if it seems well hidden at times!)

Some people enjoy this recognition, while others appear to shy away from it. The latter are often afraid that somehow their inner being can be hurt by others if it is perceived. This is a fallacy. The personality and the body can be hurt by others, but not the innermost being. For this is pure essence, energy and light. It can be covered and hidden, but not destroyed.

## Communication

In the vastness of your experience, there are some areas which cause you much pain. One of these is your communicating with each other. Communication is a delicate dance between different beings, requiring much skill and manoeuvring. More often than not it tends to reduce love between the parties. This is not the way it could be, or was, intended.

The following little story shows how this so often happens:

There was a woman who went to an older woman asking for advice. The older woman asked who she was, to which the younger replied 'I am your younger sister.' The older woman was taken by surprise and asked how that could be. The younger woman replied 'You and I are one'. The older woman was becoming more astonished. 'Who are you?' she asked again.

'I am you'. replied the younger woman.

The older woman thought about this and finally said 'We do not know each other. And how can you be who I am? There is only one of me.'

To which the reply was 'We are all one'.

We see here a complete lack of communication. Perhaps the women are both right, but neither is able to explain to or convince the other. They are virtually coming from different dimensions. This is how it is in your world. You are all one, yet you are at a range of different levels of understanding, which makes genuine communication very difficult for you. What we see is so much conflict due to differing views, rather than due to one being right and the other wrong. The key to your success here is, as we see it, for you to communicate clearly and with much patience and desire to understand the other. Otherwise, you may well miss each other and unnecessary conflict may eventuate.

## Silence is golden

To move onto a slightly different area, we now wish to speak about silence. When two or more people gather in silence, there is much potential for interaction between them. This is because words are an ego function and so often create division, no matter how well intentioned. Many of your places of worship would have more success in helping people connect to their creator and each other if their services were held in silence. It is not the words that count, but the intention. A congregation with the intention of connection, an environment conducive to it, and silence, would be better off than one with the best preacher in the world. Preaching moves the head all too often, not the heart. Connection is a function of the heart mainly. How many preachers talk of 'opening up your heart to the Lord', while so busy engaging their congregations' heads with words that they cannot possibly do it?

Try more silence in your relationships. Peaceful, connected silence, that is. Wars and arguments were never caused by silence, but by words or actions. Too many words are rashly spoken and later regretted when they cannot be withdrawn.

Silence has become deeply unfashionable in your world. Anyone too quiet is probed, questioned and eventually at risk of being sent to the doctor! We urge you to change the way you look upon silence. It is needed for centering yourselves, for reflection and re-evaluation, as well as for connection.

Now on to more practical matters. We do not wish you to think we are some kind of cosmic 'know-alls'. We, like you, have made what we would consider some mistakes. We, too, have much to learn. However, we are more practised at what you need to learn at this time. This is why we are helping you now. Our strengths are love, peace, relating, creating and harmony overall. These are what your planet lacks. Until you have learnt what you need to learn in order to evolve to the next stage, we will be with you in one form or another. This is for all of our sakes.

Begin somewhere. Just choose one way in which you might change, and start there. To change one small habit is better than to change nothing at all. Once one change has been incorporated, start on another. Gradually, much can be accomplished. But go easy on yourself. Do not expect yourself or others to change overnight. This leads to discouragement and abandonment of the goal.

# Leadership

If you are in a position of authority over others, you may be in a position to make significant changes for many people. Anyone in a leadership role would do well to examine his style of leadership. Does it conform to society's economic expectations entirely, or does it serve mankind better than this? Are people recognised and listened to? Is there a place for silence? Are the values promoted ones that will further the well-being of the human race as a whole, or are they based on local perceived need, to the detriment of the whole? We challenge you, the leaders of government and industry, to put these questions to yourselves, and seek an honest answer. Most of your solutions have been short-term, local ones. Remember, the local population is a part of the whole population of your Earth, and due to the collective nature of the organism, will be greatly affected by the fate of the whole. A small slice of the population cannot be seen in isolation in realistic terms. You all share the one planet, and what affects the one affects the other.

We ask you, the leaders, to imagine your company, your government, running its business without a world as you know it. Is the priority really to look after the profits of the company at the expense of the environment? Would you rather have a huge salary package in a dirty world, or a moderate salary in a beautiful world? Would you rather see a big balance in your bank account now, or a healthy world for your grandchildren?

We ask you, the leaders of governments, corporations, small business and families, to remember who you are. You are not your cars, your holidays, your portfolios, your titles, your goods and chattels. These are all the outer trappings of the real you. You are actually the same as that starving beggar, as that unemployed father, as that amputee, as that child. You are ultimately a divine spark. The fact that you have perhaps come into a position of power over others does not for one moment mean that you are any more worthy or deserving than they. Each is but a small but potent cog in the wheel of life on your Earth, and the bigger the role in decision-making, the more carefully and responsibly the role needs to be carried out for the ultimate good of the whole.

Leadership has too often come to be tied up with money and influence, rather than wisdom and kindness. Once in the position of power the ego often becomes inflated and goes to great lengths in order to retain the position, even at the cost of conscience. To complicate matters further, many of the apparent leaders are not in effect the leaders, for they are dictated to behind the scenes by industrial and commercial bodies more economically powerful. This is a very tricky problem for many leaders of government. Even those with a strong social conscience are sorely tried by the economics of it all. Please bear in mind that money is nothing more than a social construct and should not be the basis for decision-making, when weighed up against the long term well-being of humankind.

CHAPTER 10

# If it is to be, it's up to me...

## Powerlessness and responsibility

Personal responsibility is a term which is popular in your personal development circles. This is appropriate, as we see it, and particularly now. At this time there is a great feeling of powerlessness in many of you. It seems to you as though you are getting swept away in a tide not of your making. Decisions made by politicians you elected seem to bear little or no relationship to the promises made before the elections. Many of you feel an edge of disappointment and disillusionment with the system. Trust has worn thin..

## Common wishes

We are here to tell you that you are not powerless. You can change the tide. If enough of you care and you act, you can reverse many of the trends you see happening. Perhaps you are not aware how many of you, worldwide, share the same concerns. You are a mighty force, if employed properly. You have allowed your countries' boundaries to separate you in space and in thought, but there is much that unites you.

All over your world, people want liberty. You know you were born to have free will, and the curtailment of this in any way feels unacceptable to you. All over your world is a desire that no one should starve or be killed in war. Everywhere is the wish for the Earth to continue to function as a beautiful and bountiful host for you, as she does now. Everyone in your world, even the most hardened cynic, wants love.

These are huge links of intent, which can be harnessed as raw power to change contrary forces peacefully. Please be aware that whether you are in an apartment in New York, in an ashram in India or a shack in Africa, you share these desires. This is because you have an innate sense of what works for you as people, and what your real needs are. It is not too late for you to use this knowledge to advantage for your world.

## The power of intent

As humanity changes, more and more there is a direct link between your conscious intent and outcomes. In other words, you are more able to create your future realities than ever before. As you evolve, there is a more direct relationship between your thoughts and matter. You are approaching the realm of causality as a collective. So whereas what we are telling you now would not have been relevant for most of you a hundred years ago, it is absolutely relevant now. Please believe you have powers most of your grandparents would not have dreamt of. It is time to put these powers into action for the benefit of all mankind.

## Visualising the future (exercise)

What we ask you to do is simple. Once per day, put down your work, your shopping, your talking, and for a few minutes visualise how your world could be ideally. See a globe of great beauty, peace and health, cared for by beings of love and joy. Picture people and animals well fed, happy and harmonious. Picture caring world governments of holistic awareness, solving any disagreements amicably, with reason and understanding. Visualise the Earth's body and soul restoring itself as no further damage takes place.

Do not be perturbed if you cannot see a way for this to really occur on Earth. Create the picture, and the means to manifest it will follow. That it how it works.

If one million people on Earth did this for ten minutes each day, the tide would turn. You have so much power. Can you imagine what would happen if everywhere on Earth schools held just one minute's silence daily for pupils to visualise a better world? If factories and offices stopped in shifts for five minutes a day? If 10 million people per day visualised? This is a small percentage of your population worldwide, but it would make a striking difference, quickly. Even if, at this stage, you do not feel convinced enough to try it, please keep this idea in mind, for there may come a time when you will.

We so urgently want you to understand and believe the power of this simple technique. In order to test it out, we suggest you try it in the family or social situation you find yourself in. Pick a relationship you have with someone and imagine that relationship being just as great as it could be. See it for a few minutes each day. And watch the changes after a few weeks, or even before that. One person's efforts have less effect than millions, but millions are only made up of single people after all.

There are already numbers of you aware of these concepts, and using them. To you we say: you are so needed at this time. Please keep up what you are doing. It is having effect. Never doubt that. If it were not for your efforts, your world would be in a worse shape now.

Your world is in a state of waiting, for the cycle to end and change to come. It is up to you whether the change that comes is manageable or not. You can be swept along on the tide of past patterns and possibly carried over the waterfall's edge, or you can build a raft of vision and steer it together to a safe and beautiful shore. It is up to you, each one of you.

We cannot do it for you. We cannot swoop in and rescue you from fates you have created. That is beyond our briefing. Your free will takes precedence. We can only inform and advise. The action is for you to take.

CHAPTER 11

# To the end of time...

## Man's mission on earth

Your mission was to be the experiential dimension of your creator. This you have done flawlessly. You have experienced as wide a range of emotions, actions and adventures as anyone could wish for.

This phase is now completing itself. Your mission is about to change.

## Light and shadow

Long ago there was a God who loved. That was all she did. She loved so strongly that her love split into many particles, which became all of us. (This is a little simplified, but we want to make a point.) She watched these souls and loved them, experiencing her love afresh through each of them. As they progressed, she saw herself in them – her light and her dark, her day and her night. How could she have light without dark, or dark without light? The two were clearly inseparable. She had given the Earthlings free will, knowing that behind light was always a shadow. She saw this shadow emerge in their lives and play a part. She saw it keeping a balance.

## Man's creation of evil

Yet, man was disquieted by the darkness and was not able to reconcile it with his light. He gradually pushed it away from himself until it became a separate force. This is the force that man has learnt to call Satan, the devil, evil or the anti-Christ. Man has always seen it as separate from God, and has thus empowered it to unbalance his world.

The time has now come for man to reintegrate the dark with the light, and thus regain the balance. This is one of the reasons for so much racial hatred and violence, so much crime, murder and the polarisation of left and right. It is a final separating of dark and light before they once again merge into peaceful balance.

## Light dissolves shadow

This will be a gradual process and will be eased by your understanding that this is what is happening. Please bear in mind that of themselves the dark forces have no power. They have been given power by man's fears. The way to overcome them is always with love. This they cannot tolerate because they automatically become bound to it, as they were originally. The stronger and more authentic the love, the less the dark forces can resist.

We are by no means telling you to condone the actions of evil that occur from time to time, but that collectively, the force of love on your planet can overcome the force of evil. Again, this is up to each of you. Whoever you are, your love counts in the collective world army against darkness. If you are unemployed, or very young, or poor, your contribution can be as great as anyone's to change the world peacefully.

The sooner the forces are reunited, the less trauma you will need to undergo. It is a process that has begun, and the struggle is on. Dark forces prefer separation; love unites and love is the stronger of the two ultimately. Once the two forces are linked, you will have an endless, wonderfully peaceful age.

Another side of this to remember is that you are not made to begin wars, but to end them.

What we mean by this is that your skills lie more in joining forces than dividing them. This is because you are at heart beings of love. That is your essence. So, until you remember who you are, you will have unnecessary divisions amongst yourselves, which later will not occur.

It is time for the revolution of the soul. Your souls have been going through many different phases – some more constructive than others. Now they are ready to take on their original mission again, but in a new and different way – with conscious love. Love, as we have stated, has always been the basis of your matter, but this has not been known by you at a conscious level. Your religions have tried to get this across to you, but have done so through messengers who could not grasp the full extent of it themselves. Thus has the knowledge, given to a few, been distorted to suit politics of the day.

You are now at an extraordinary turning point, in which you will at last understand the real force, power and meaning of love, and its complete relevance to you. Once this stage has been reached, there will be a change in the way you organise your world, and a turning away from destructiveness. The forces of light will triumph. This is one possible scenario – the one we hope you will create. The others would be less fortunate for us all, and we hope you will avert these by believing us and following our suggestions.

Following this train of thought, please do not believe there is 'no easy way'. There is. The ideal is the easiest; the straightest line between two points is the shortest. However, we do not necessarily mean the easiest in the short term. We speak of the easiest overall, in the bigger, long-term picture. For many of you it has become the norm that you will do whatever seems quickly effective. You have lost your sense of patience and perseverance. This is a pity, but these are habits you are capable of changing.

Our discussion earlier about focussing on fixing the present is one we need to return to now. We are not talking here about short-term solutions. A solution should be one that helps the present, but also leads in the direction of a consciously chosen future. This does not include worrying about the future.

We are fast approaching a potentially marvellous time for you on Earth. The choice is yours: work towards this now, or allow another future to take its course.

## Eating habits

Towards this same end, we would ask you not to

become complacent about your habits in general. What you eat, what you do, what you say, all define the direction of your world. It may seem irrelevant to you what you decide to have for breakfast, but it is not. By eating fruit, for instance, as opposed to egg and bacon, you are achieving quite a number of things.

Firstly, you are not adding to the growing number of carnivores. Eating meat has a few intrinsic problems in terms of your evolution. Meat lowers your vibrational rate, which makes it more difficult for you to evolve. Grazing, as you know, is denuding your lands, as well as ultimately causing fear and pain to a large number of creatures. This fear and pain is a part of your own. It is around you and influences you more than you realise.

Secondly, is the issue of intensity. Meat, on one hand, fuels aggression; while fruit and vegetables do not. There is the problem of chemical contamination in all your foods now. That is at present unavoidable, and certainly undesirable in terms of your well-being. However, it is not as serious as some may surmise. Far more threatening to you is the effect of eating meat.

Many of you are allowing yourselves to go down a slippery slide in terms of your eating habits. Your bodies are exquisite machines, which, like the Earth, can self-regulate to a large extent. However, there are lengths beyond which they cannot go. It is unrealistic to expect your bodies to tolerate the lack of nutrition and surplus of toxins you pump in to them. Most of you look after your dogs and cats better than yourselves, in terms of diet. Because you have made your water unpalatable, you ingest a variety of chemical concoctions, supposedly to hydrate the body. These only further dehydrate you, and add to the toxic load of chemicals, which you expect your body to deal with.

You may wonder why you are stressed and tired, often blaming it on your work. The healthy human body and mind is made to be capable of very taxing work and thought. It is only when you allow yourselves to become run-down that you become stressed by the demands of daily life. When your car starts to falter, you take it for a tune-up, but when *you* flag, all too often you reach for some more junk food. Your mind and soul are magical and unlimited, but your body is only a well-designed machine – a vehicle, like your car. So be kinder to it, for you still need it for some time to come.

## Actions invite responses

Your actions provide the stimulus for others to respond to. If you do not always get the responses you want from others, or from life in general, study your actions. Your actions in the present form the direction of the future, just as your thoughts do. Look at what options of response you are allowing others and the universe in general when you act.

Your thoughts, feelings, speech and actions together form a pathway upon which your destiny travels. In other words, they ultimately create your destiny. Form for yourselves light destinies, through actions which benefit each other. There is no need to scrabble to get your needs met. There is enough of everything you need for all of you on Earth. As we have said, it is only a matter of distribution, and this relies on your sound actions, based on sound thought.

If you were to forget your monetary system and take stock of your real goods, you would find that many of you had a surplus and many a lack. How easy this would be to rectify if you had no fear getting in the way of logic. Would you be afraid of the 'unfairness' of someone getting something for nothing? What about the unfairness of never having the opportunity to earn something at all? The concept of fairness needs to be addressed on a global level, as it is seen out of perspective when seen in isolation on a personal level.

What you say does count in the scheme of things. Words may not be visible to you, unless written down, but they affect matter, as they are made of thought. The underlying intent of speech is more effective than the words actually used, as many of you know. The intent is the thought, and this holds the power. So use your words carefully and wisely, to have a positive effect.

## Conscious speech and thought

The more consciously you choose your thoughts, words and actions, the more of your power you are exercising. If you are not consciously choosing, you are allowing your unconscious desires to rule, and are inviting outcomes not of your choosing. Thus are you swept along unknowingly by the tide, likely to find yourself washed up on unchosen shores.

This is what has happened collectively to humankind so far, and this is one way to view the cause of your problems. We are pleased to now see a strong movement towards greater consciousness amongst you, and it is due to this that we are now able to help you.

By the time you have reached full consciousness, all that we are telling you will have become quite irrelevant to you. This is because you will be beyond needing such information; and because you will be able to tap into complete knowledge yourselves.

CHAPTER 12

# And so it was...

## There are no standards

Before time began you were not expected to do anything. You are still not expected to do any particular thing. There is no one judging you, for all we have said. We and others may be observing, but there is no one passing judgement on your worth as beings, based on your actions, or lack thereof. There is no standard. This is something you have forgotten. There is no rule book. There are just thoughts, decisions, actions and consequences. And there are those of us watching who can see the consequences perhaps more clearly than you can.

Please remember that in the beginning it was not like this. We all started off together as one undivided spark. Shortly after that we parted and went our separate ways. Then it was that our experiences started to differ, due to the influence of our different locations. At the same time, various clusters were forming throughout space, which became host to many different beings.

Over time, some of these beings developed advanced technology, others evolved in terms of their souls, and still others specialised in love. We are of the latter group and you are of the middle group.

## The great remembering

Your souls have evolved to rainbow depths due to your experiences. The problem is that you have become disconnected consciously from your souls. They are like underground rivers, pulsing with life, but unattainable and invisible to you. The exercises given to you in this book are about reconnecting with your souls. They are to help you regain your power and knowledge.

Please understand that we are not here to judge. We love you and want you to see yourselves for the grand beings that you are. Each of you is endlessly magnificent, but most of you cannot see this.

You are on the edge of discovering this. It will be a time of great joy and celebration when you are able to see yourselves as you really are.

This is the beginning of the return of your memory. You will begin to experience snatches of who you are, of what you can do. You will be excited and may be incredulous. Those of you who have these experiences early would be wise not to disclose too much to others who may not be ready. However, to share your discoveries with others of like mind will be most important.

As you remember who you are, you will start to accept who we are. This is happening now. There have been many clues given to and received by you, about us and others like us. Please remember, at least

we are family. At most we are one. We all came from the same spark. So although you may be more drawn to some than to others, we suggest you treat all beings you meet with respect and love. There will be no need for violence against any being. The strongest weapon against darkness is light. Light is love. So use love to disempower any dark forces you might meet, and use discrimination in deciding on your actions. Love does not mean submission, and love does not mean agreement. Love means connection. To send love to a being means to connect that being to its source. When a being is connected to its source, it can no longer do harm.

## Choosing your future

Prior to you reaching the next stage there will be many changes, some of which will be easier than others for you to cope with. Identify with the ones that seem positive and deny those which do not lead in hopeful directions. What we mean by 'deny' is: do not give credence to, do not invest your belief into. Do not count them in your future in a deep sense. See any destructive situations as anomalies, as temporary breaks from the pattern of things, rather than the start of new and unpleasant patterns. This will help to end these phases soon, rather than feeding their strength.

This is how evolution works. That which is seen as important and is identified with, becomes incorporated into the pattern of the future, and that which is seen as just a short-term anomaly becomes exactly that, and ultimately insignificant.

This truth accounts for man being as he is today.

What he has stressed as a collective has become more of a reality. However, it is more complex than this. Within the greater collective, you have smaller ones – groups with various interests and purposes at heart. Each of these has influence on the greater whole, depending on how strong and clear its intent is, not necessarily on the magnitude of its membership.

Numbers do not actually count for much in your world. What actually dictates the course of events is the power of intent. Ten people with clear and determined intent can have far more effect than a hundred who are drifting along with vague aims. Had you understood this, you might not have given your dictators as much power. Resistance in anger is energy wasted. Anger and other unhappy emotions dilute power. If you wish to change a course of events, become completely clear on the alternative you want, and think, talk and work towards it. Many of your leaders are good at developing clear, strong and unemotional intent. This is one of the ways they achieve what they do in your societies. One person like this can easily have power over hundreds of indecisive people.

## Aiding your leaders

In the past you as a collective have tended to give the power to your leaders, and then grumbled about their mismanagement. A more helpful way would be to give them the nominal power, if that is your system of choice, then help them make wise decisions, by envisioning a chosen future every day for yourselves.

A leader is in a difficult and confusing position – torn between fixing past problems, aiming for what seems to be constructive change, and often protecting the interests of his own ego and position, which often includes protecting or competing against colleagues. In order to come to decisions, your leaders must gather information from a range of sources. Their antennas are out, in a sense, to receive information on all the relevant topics. Some comes from the media, some from their advisers and other outward sources, but do not under-estimate how much the consciousness of their people influences them. In their minds they are pulled many different ways by your thoughts. How they respond to all these influences depends partly on the strength of their egos, partly on their soul connection, partly on the perceived invulnerability of their positions.

If you continue to caretake your world in the way you have been, how do you see your future? If the world was a house, you were the owner and the tenant was treating your house as man has treated the Earth, would you renew the lease?

We ask for your serious consideration of these matters, for your sake and ours.

You are at a momentous cliff edge of time – one in which your decisions could cause you to fall or fly. We hope you will choose to fly.

CHAPTER 13

# Revolutions.

## Earth cycles

Throughout your history there have been cycles. Your progress has never been linear, though you have tried to see it in this way. You have constantly evolved through revolving, returning to a different level of the same spot. Imagine now, if you will, that while you have been doing this, around you Earth has been going through her cycles, too. Not just the night and day, tidal and seasonal cycles, but greater patterns.

These Earth cycles have to do with magnetism. Just as your magnetic fields are affected by the cycles of Earth, so are Earth's affected by other galactic forces.

## Spirit and matter

There are two main types of creation – essence or spirit, and matter.

Your souls are made of spirit; Earth and your bodies are of matter. Matter is bound by certain natural laws, whereas spirit is free to reinvent itself more or less, and can affect matter.

## Man as caretaker

Earth is approaching a time when her own magnetic field will change. This will impact to some extent upon all her tenants. Man, being the self-appointed caretaker, is in a position to make the transition more bearable for the other species on Earth. Or he may speed up their destruction in this possibly difficult time.

## What really counts

Before the change happens, man needs to know where his priorities lie. If many species are to survive, you, collectively, need to be very clear on what you really value, before that time. If it is money and goods, you will steer yourselves towards certain outcomes; if it is humanity and your environment, you will make other choices. We urge you to clarify within yourself what matters to you.

In order to help you clarify your values, let us look at a few possible scenarios:

- Here is a supermarket, packed to the ceiling with delectable synthetic foods, all for the taking. Next door is a huge department store, full of household and recreational goods, clothing, even cars, all for you to help yourself. Outside is cement, and beyond that, bare ground. There are no trees, plants, birds, pets – only buildings. No matter how far you travel, you will not be able to find a flower, a blade of grass, or a piece of natural fruit.

- Here is a marketplace where people go to trade or sell goods. There is not a big variety, but whatever is there is useful and healthy. Beyond the marketplace there are lawns, trees and you can hear birdsong. Buildings are simple, with greenery between, and no matter how far afield you travel, you will not find a beggar, for everyone has food and a home.

• Here is a rich man's house. Inside are luscious fruits grown by servants, in a greenhouse. The fabrics in the house are beautiful and opulent. Music is played by a quintet as the owner lies sipping an exotic drink. Around the house is a very high wall, topped with barbs and broken glass. Its purpose is to keep out the hordes of hungry, wailing, hot people who have no food or shelter.

These are some of the possible scenarios for your future, which already have their seeds in the present.

Which would you prefer?

Which will you create?

It is likely that you would be divided amongst yourselves as to what you would choose. In the future this division will in all probability escalate. Groups will gather and form bigger groups, until there are only a few main factions. This is when your greatest conflicts may arise. It is then that your mind power will be so needed to tip the balance. So develop the power of your minds and intent before that time. We believe that most of the people concerned with doing so will also be concerned with the survival and order of life on earth. This training will give them a head start.

There are endless pieces to the jigsaw. In this book we are providing you with glimpses of a few, which we hope will assist you to gain clarity of vision. The pieces of the jigsaw are more interlinked than they might at first appear. Let us explain further, with some necessary repetition:

Earth is heading for a cyclical change. Man lives on Earth, and has always been affected by his surroundings. If you live in a stuffy house there is less oxygen and you are less alert. If you live in a house in which there has been much joy, you sense this and it affects you to a greater or lesser extent, usually quite unconsciously. If you live on a world that is on the brink of change, you will be on the brink of change too.

Earth's change is Mankind's change. However, there is another strong interdependence, which you need to understand. Man cannot stop Earth's change. That is a cycle beyond his control. He therefore cannot prevent his own change, for he must adapt in some way to his environment shifting. He does, however, have much power to assist not only himself and his fellow occupants, but Earth herself. One could almost say that man could be Earth's midwife in this situation. It depends largely on man whether Earth gives birth to a future of beauty or of pain.

This will be the first great Earth cycle to take place with man's conscious knowledge. Yet, it is receiving less attention in most countries than the favourite sport. Scientists and metaphysicians are pointing to the same likelihoods, and governments are turning away, to their economic balance sheets. They do not know what to do. We do not judge them, but we wish they would wake up in time.

None of you would wish for some of the scenarios we see gathering force in your future. As we have said, we do not wish by any means to frighten you, but to wake you up to your situation in time.

Please, go about your business as usual, if that is what you wish to do, but include in your routine just a few minutes a day to think about these matters – not to worry, but to gain clarity about your hopes for the future.

There are among you those who would devote your lives to the cause if you knew what to do. If that desire is so strong, you will be shown what to do within your capabilities. Remain open to ideas and flexible in terms of lifestyle. For it is not long before you will be thrust into the action one way or another. It may not be of your choosing, but it will eventuate.

## Responding to change

All the warnings and knowledge we can give you may not amount to much in the light of information you have passed between yourselves for hundreds of years; but our perception is that more of you are open to different views now than ever before, and that there is a global disillusionment with the status quo. This being the case, take heed. Listen to your intuition, for it is that which speaks to you through your disappointment and uncertainty. It is asking you to seek a new direction – to turn the next revolution.

Do not be afraid of change, for you have lived with it

all your lives. The only reason to fear change is if you doubt your ability for consciously chosen response. For your response is all that ultimately matters. To respond is to give an event credence by recognising it through a return event. If you are responding from a position of fear, it is more difficult for you to hear what your soul wants; in other words for you to respond with integrity.

In times of stress, it is easy to respond from the ego, which is often far removed from the soul. These are the times to be particularly cautious about your actions and words. Be on your guard against sudden rushes of anger, blame and invigorating competition. For these are the fuel of division and separation and, we suggest, the enemies of your chosen future. It might feel safer to prove yourself to be above a threatening party, but this means you have reduced the other into an inferior position, and it is these positions which seem to create most aggression in your world.

## Short-term solutions

Before we speak more about change and dealing with it, we would like you to take note of one small factor which has a hidden cost: Most of mankind has developed a habit of seeing only what is closest to its nose. It is no coincidence that so many of you develop shortsightedness by middle age.

It is wise not to react until you have also thought about the longer term implications. The short term is always easier to see, but the hidden cost of following its dictates can be huge. It often takes you away from your true direction, or your soul's chosen direction, later entailing a slow and arduous return.

Short-term decisions take place in relationships and on national and international scale. How many people find themselves unhappily married because it was 'a good idea at the time'. It was convenient, the relationship was already there, everyone else seemed to be getting married at that age and, besides, the physical closeness was comforting and exciting. For so many of you, a short-term view on marriage has led to years of unpleasantness and misery. If you had approached marriage in a different way, you might have waited longer, but in return enjoyed many years of fulfilment.

Countries in conflict are often very blinkered to the longer term outcomes when they choose war as a way to get what they want. They might get what they want, – or lose it and more – but at what horrendous cost to both sides. Does it make sense to sacrifice so many of the next generation for the sake of more land, or the implementation of policies? We cannot see it this way. Whether a country is the winner' or 'loser' in a war, it often takes generations to rebuild, not only the physical structures but the psychological balance of its occupants. There can be no doubt that everyone loses in such a case.

The only long term way to solve conflict is through love. How can separation be the answer to separation? If the problem is separation, the solution must be joining together. It is so obvious, yet most of mankind is too caught in fears and ancient conditioning to see it.

So be wary of short-term thinking. It is a far greater danger to you than other perceived threats, such as lack or differences.

Now to move on to other themes relating to change:

## Karma in decline

You may or may not believe in karma. It is a concept hardly relevant to you anymore, but convenient in terms of explaining certain laws of the universe. We would like you to know that karma is coming to an end in your world. This means that you are no longer obliged to live out the past, in a sense. It will soon be a time of living purely in response to the present moment, in full consciousness.

At present, much of your consciousness is tied up with issues of your involvement in other times or spaces, enabling you only to see rather skewed versions of your present. Believe us, this is changing fast. This could be why so many of you are amazed when what you want almost instantly appears in some form or another. It is as though you had been in shackles which are now being released.

Although this should be a time of celebration for you, we see many of you frightened and confused by the changes. You are not yet able to trust their validity. This is a pity. We would say to you: trust that what is happening in this way is for the best and is, in fact, most liberating for you. Once you have realised what is happening and are able to surrender to the process, you will be able to appreciate the peace and freedom it brings you.

## Natural ecstasy

Another matter which needs clarifying is the one of ecstasy. Ecstasy is not a state most of you can indulge in at will at present. This is one of the reasons for your drug problems. Paradise has seemed so illusive to you that many of you have sought its equivalent in chemicals. This is unnecessary. There are ways for you to experience ecstasy which are perfectly harmless and easy to attain. It is all about being in a true state of balance. The natural state of the human being is ecstatic. It is only when you lose your natural balance that you lose your joy. So, if you find ways to regain your balance, through lifestyle, spiritual or metaphysical means, you will regain your natural delight in living, and drugs will be no longer desirable.

Remember, please, that Earth is your home. It is for you to decide and dictate what happens here. It is imperative that you have all your wits about you to make these decisions. They cannot be wisely made by a people who are side-tracked by political motivations, drugged with desires, or semi-conscious from distractions. This is the only present you have in which to focus on what matters to you as a people. What you decide today creates the world of tomorrow. We know you have heard this before, but we cannot stress enough how important this message is.

Every revolution or evolution runs its course and how it affects people largely depends on their reaction to it. There are many possible outcomes of the next major change. It all depends on you.

CHAPTER 14

# The times they are a-changing…

## Anything is possible

Do not believe everything you read. You often read about the future in sad, prophetic terms. How El Nino may become a permanent phenomenon, causing droughts, tidal waves, fires, floods and famine; how your world is perched on the edge of nuclear or biological warfare; how deforestation and foreign electromagnetic radiations are escalating and racial polarisation is increasing. These may all be likely scenarios should you do nothing to stop them. Certainly their seeds have been planted. However, there are now many different levels of influence occurring in your world.

No longer do the actions on the physical plane overpower those on the mental plane. You have moved up the ladder, so to speak, and the thoughts and intentions you hold now exert more power than in the past. Even though there are existent situations to overcome, if you know what you want to create, and send that message out firmly and clearly to the absolute – the place of absolute power and stillness – your message will be heard and responded to.

In a situation which seems hopeless, either because of existing conditions, or because you perceive that you have little influence, this is the best way to go about achieving change. The reason is that your visions of possibility are usually limited by what you know, whereas in the absolute there is no limitation – anything at all is possible. Remember, limitations only exist in your minds, and because of this you manifest them.

There are no limitations in reality.

## Will and ego

Much stress has been placed, in your business and personal development circles, on setting goals, being dynamic and 'making things happen'. These concepts have their limitations, as they are all ego-based. They are all based on using the will to create an impact upon the environment.

## Tuning into the absolute

The human will and ego are restricted by their very natures. A far more efficient way of effecting change is to go through the absolute. It is, in effect, stepping up your power and adding a quality of limitlessness to the problem-solving possibilities and outcomes.

At this time you are amassing great quantities of knowledge suddenly, which are often difficult for you to integrate with your lifestyles. Do not let this worry you. You will gradually find ways to use the knowledge you are receiving. Do not attempt to make shifts in your lives too suddenly and impulsively.

You need to achieve some stability within your new knowledge before you will know how to use it wisely. So be circumspect. This does not mean shelving what you are learning. No, by all means apply it to your present situation. And as opportunities for change in your lives arise, which will lead to more congruence with your new goals, take them. If the changes are to be successful, then the process needs to be a gradual one. Yet, it will still seem very quick to you.

## Life is change

Remember, too, that you are made to keep changing. It is the cyclical nature of your world. Nothing is ever truly in stasis. Even when dead, your matter goes through the cycle of decomposition. Even rocks are constantly changing in response to their environment and conditions. Change is inescapable, and to deny it is futile and exhausting.

It is a difficult world for you now, but it was not so originally. You have in a sense, turned your globe into the enemy, through repeatedly abusing it and each other. A rebellious child can only rebel so much before the family is no longer a happy, harmonious unit. This is how it works within the cause and effect system you have created. Over time, that child separates himself so much from his family that he is, in fact, only rebelling against himself. This is what leads him to eventually see himself, and to change one way or another.

## Rationality and the unconscious

Within your system of controls, checks and

balances, you all seem to know what you are doing. But may we put it to you that very few of you have any idea of where you are headed and of how you are really affecting those around you. It seems to us that you are somewhat out of control. Because you are not fully conscious in your choices, you are not fully in control. However, many of you would be surprised at this, believing the rational mind to be the most suitable and safe decision-maker. This is not the case.

The rational mind has its place in the scheme of things, but it does not have access to very much knowledge. It is like a computer. It is fed information and can then make decisions based on this information. New thought does not come from the rational mind. One could describe it as a processor and no more. A significant part of the processing of information is the filtering applied by the subconscious mind. This influences the interpretation of data, based on prior experiences and perceptual sets. Now, when you believe you are basing decisions on purely rational thought, you are usually completely denying this process of filtering, which accounts for a great deal of distortion.

For example, in reading this, you may be receiving many different versions of what we are saying, coloured by your prior knowledge, value systems and perceptions. It is therefore not valid to say there is one version of the truth. The truth is always relative to the subjective. What we are trying to say is that there is no right way to behave in your world, no right way to think or feel. There are only millions of possibilities, open to you by virtue of the fact that you seek them.

As soon as you believe you have found one way that is the right one, the other possibilities temporarily close down to you. That is how it works and that is something most of you do not understand.

There is, therefore, no sense in dictating to oneself or others, for there is no yardstick. We have tried to explain this to you in several ways. It is a concept deeply lost to most of you, through the misguided efforts of your religions, governments, schools and parenting. But it still holds true. You probably see the apparent discrepancy in what we are saying. There are no truths, but this is true! The only way we can explain this to you is that the absolute is absolute. In other words I AM is perhaps the only truth there is. Beyond this, all is flexible. This is the great experiment.

In your computer games you have created a mirror of your reality. The player chooses various actions and when he does, the other paths close down. Many of your games are based on violence, reflecting your life games, and many of them end in death, as your lives seem to, to you. How interesting and ironic that so many of the generation who have created these games, based on their own lives, despise the violence they see their children perpetrating on them.

## Stress management versus change

You have reached a sort of implosion, in which you are turning on each other, as you turned on the Earth. This implosion is fuelled by the stress you have caused yourselves, through valuing separation, competition and materialism. Your world does not need stress management. It needs a major review in terms of the paths you have chosen to travel.

What we most want you to understand is that the choice is always yours. Believe in the path you have chosen, and it will continue to unravel in the direction it is headed, which does not look too favourable to us. Or deny the relevance of this path and venture on to another. No paths have been closed permanently to you. Their potential is always still there.

To return to the discussion of the rational mind: be aware that there are other more effective ways of gathering information and making decisions. It has long been a vague dream of mankind that there is ultimate, complete knowledge out there for you to tap into, if only you knew how. There is talk of Akashic records and intuitive knowing. This dream has fed that path of reality, until now there are large numbers of you who find that you can, in fact, gain access to this total knowledge. For many of you this only happens in glimpses as yet, but it nevertheless happens. It could only happen because the possibility of it was in your consciousness.

The basic law of how this works has never changed. It is your understanding that is shifting, and therefore your power to make use of this law. We are trying every way we know how to explain to you that you are floating in a sea of possibilities – some horrific, some mediocre and some absolutely beautiful. You are drifting at present in a current of your own making towards the less favourable ones. We do not wish to see this happen and cannot actively intervene unless invited by you. We sincerely hope that you will become conscious enough to avert the future you are currently creating and the regret that would surely follow.

If you were to relinquish your belief in time as a concept, there would be no urgency. For as long as you are within time, there is a limit to the time you have left before your current path unfolds towards unfavourable futures. We aim to express this urgency to you, without alarming you into inaction.

There are never too many factors militating against change. Change is always possible as long as it is deemed so, and, as we have said, it is inevitable. To go from forward into reverse in a car simply means changing gears. The workings of the gears do not have to concern the driver – that is all taken care of. The driver merely has to have the intent of changing gear and act on it, and it is done. That is the simple mechanics of your world. You do not need to understand how the changes are made to happen; you do not have to force them. Merely make the decision and act on it in some way, as a sign of your intent being serious. That action may mean no longer supporting an aspect of the old system, or in may mean starting a process to support the new decision. The action is, in fact, less important than the thought. It is merely a symbol of your commitment to the thought.

How many of the events that happen to you were truly planned by your conscious mind? We are sure that daily you receive surprises – not only the weather, but phone calls, chance meetings, opportunities and disappointments. And, yet, you still hold a collective belief that you can plan your day and things will go according to that plan.

This is another area of much confusion. You have learnt that you create your own reality, and so you set five-yearly, annual, weekly and daily goals and wonder why your plans so often go awry. It is because you are trying to force the river to change direction before you have made friends with the water. You are trying to use mind power without the support of the underlying power of connection. Mind power by itself is dangerous. It often lacks wisdom, and steamrolls its way against the natural order, leading to short-term success and long-term disaster. Another problem it causes is a sort of addiction to itself. You begin to feel more powerful after the short-term success, leading to more of the same behaviour. Others in your path who may be more connected, are flattened in your drive of determination and motivation, and ultimately you all lose.

This is not what we mean by creating your own ideal reality. The best way is to become informed before making a decision. The way to become informed is to be open to all relevant information. This is the most challenging part for most of you. As we have explained, most of you are only open to the information that fits the grids of what you already know. To allow yourself access to new information takes either courage or grace. These two can overcome the ego – the boss of the human race collectively and individually at this time. It is very hard for most of you to raise enough sustained courage to overcome your egos to the extent of integrating and acting upon new information.

Therefore, the more effective way is through divine grace – an unpopular term in your times. This does not mean that if you go to a place of worship or confession you will be granted grace. It does not mean you have to have or know a religion. It simply means you have to genuinely seek to know and do what is in harmony with the natural order – that you want to be re-aligned. When you genuinely want this and are not conditional about your desire, it is granted. For that is the order of your universe – that your soul's will, when aligned with your conscious will, has ultimate power.

Your conscious will, superimposed at odds with your soul's will, is an accident waiting to happen, unless there is a change of direction. This is because your soul will always ultimately triumph.

So, dear ones, believe that you can find the 'right' way and you will. But believe it from the depths of your being, not just in your mind.

## Mind as a vehicle for soul

Your mind is only a function of your personality – like a cut-out dress on a paper doll. When peeled away, the person is still there, with more integrity than before, in a way. Your minds are tools you have learnt to use, like time, like your personas, to interact with others in your world. There are other ways of using your minds that are not about making the right impression, controlling your environment or manipulating each other. We do not say this is all you do with your minds, but it is most of what you do.

With your permission, you are entering a time when your minds will instead be a vehicle for your souls.

As your minds are influential over your treatment of your bodies, this will mean that your bodies too, will at last be treated as the vehicles for the soul. Should this possibility become a reality, you will experience the joy of total integration, and the power of complete knowledge. This is a very real possibility. There is a small, increasing tributary from your river heading this way fast, but the majority of the river is headed the other way. In every thought or action you have, you feed the tributary or the river. Over time, or should we say, over intent, the tributary could easily become larger and change the course of the whole river.

This is your choice and your task.

CHAPTER 15

# Thy will be done...

## God just is

Thanks to your religions, you probably have the belief that your God is watching over your every move, ready to pounce on the transgressor of laws he has imposed.

Nothing could be further from the truth. There is no god with a personality. God is just an absolute – a force, a power, love, an energy. Because you have defined yourselves by your personalities, you have defined god by one, which you have superimposed on it. God is not, cannot be defined in any way other than absolute.

It would be more realistic for you to view god as an electromagnetic force than as a personality. But that would still be inaccurate. God is the 'isness', you are the 'beingness'. A 'beingness' must have an 'isness' as its basis to exist. Let us examine the word ex-is-t. It implies that by departing from, we are. This is exactly how it works. But if in departing we also deny the existence of what we departed from, we lose our 'isness' and our 'beingness' becomes hollow.

We put it to you: If you knew that this was the case,

how would your lives be different? In what way would you be prepared to change the way you view your world and its contents? Our guess is that you would not be living the way you are now.

The raw materials you received were given to you as a giant playground, for you to make of whatever you wanted. You are still in that position. Only you have begun to destroy your playground fast recently. As far as god is concerned, that is fine. (We are using a small "g" in god purposely in this chapter. The big "G" is for a human name. God is not a human or subject to human rules.) God does not have an opinion. It is only the beings who can have an opinion.

God also has no will. God is a force – a pure force does not have a will. However, you have wills and so do we. It is your will you need to learn to do, not god's. Your will may come from your personality or from your soul. Whichever way you do it does not bother god. But it is bothering you, and us, because we are the ones affected.

## Wake up and remember

With the greatest possible respect and love, we would ask you to wake up and to remember. We are trying to jog your memories, to re-mind you, to stir you out of your spiritual slumbers.

Already there are strong stirrings of awakening from many corners of your world. Those awake automatically have more potential power than those still sleeping. It is highly unlikely that the trend to awaken will be reversed, so it is probably just a matter of time before you are all conscious. The problem, as we see it, is not so much *if* this will happen, as *when* it will happen.

It is as though there are two simultaneous races being run and the winner takes all. The first race is between man's affairs and the cycles of nature; and the second is between conscious and unconscious man. If conscious man wins the race against unconscious man before the 'cycles of nature versus. man's affairs' race is won, all will be well for you. If the latter race is completed first, one way or the other, it will be too late.

## Creating workable futures

In order to make this pronouncement, we look at the possible futures you have outlined for yourselves. Of course, the ones so far outlined are by no means the only possible ones. You can still formulate an endless number of possible outcomes. The ones that have been visualised the most strongly, will be the ones that come true. However, there is another factor to be aware of. There is also a matter of momentum, or channels. If the stage has been set for an outcome, there is less resistance to its occurring. For example: you could all visualise biological warfare, but nothing of the sort would eventuate until something had been put in place in your physical world to enable it to happen. That then would form the channel for the intent to travel upon.

It is not the means but the end that is actually the more important aspect. This goes counter to your folklore. Ultimately, it does not matter how and when you wake up and reunite, for ultimately you will. However, there are pleasant and unpleasant ways to get there, and we opt for the former.

## Your own will is being done

Believe in yourselves as the force in your world and you will see reality. You are the guiding light in your own world – not god or anyone else. You are the ones who can guide the ship of the world to safe harbours or into a cliff. It is your will and your spirit that is affecting your Earth.

Your will is being done. Be aware of what you will, while you can.

This seems a good place to end the book, as this is the crux of its purpose.

There may be nothing new in it for you, or it may all be new. We hope that wherever you are, in the process of awakening, it is a help to you and those with whom you interact. This is our strong wish.